Introduction

As a Howard University undergraduate student and president of the D. Parke Gibson Chapter of the Public Relations Student Society of America, my advisor Dr. Barbara Hines introduced me to Mr. Ofield Dukes, who taught the first public relations course at Howard University. He was an amazing public relations professional and was at that time starting the Washington, D.C. Chapter of the Black Public Relations Society (BPRS-DC).

From that moment, I was drawn in by not only his professionalism, but also by his sincerity and desire to make an impact on the lives of others. He quickly took me under his wing and offered me opportunities to volunteer with the Congressional Black Caucus Foundation, with the William Jefferson Clinton Presidential Inauguration, with establishing the BPRS-DC. He put me in charge of creating a BPRS-DC student/young professionals group working with another Howard Professor Dr. Sandra Wills (now Hannon) and with Howard alumna Lori George (now Billingsley). When I was given the Betsy Ann Plank Scholarship, he found my next internship which became my first full-time job upon graduation working at Arthur W. Shultz & Associates, a real powerhouse boutique agency at the time in D.C.

Ofield then encouraged me to have faith in God and in my abilities, and encouraged me to pursue my masters and my doctorate. He supported my doctoral studies and when I took a journalism history course, I wrote a paper about him that won an award at the American Journalism Historians Association national conference. In researching the paper, I interviewed him and he began recording himself on tapes. And I promised that I would write his entire biography.

However, life got the best of me and the biography didn't come. What did come was his autobiography and while he sent it to many of his mentees, he asked me to edit it and to ensure it was published. And now seven years later—a year of completion—it is being published.

I feel honored to have been his mentee, to have been entrusted with his memories and wisdom. And so, as you read, know that all of this is from him. Where you see footnotes, these are points I added along with my Syracuse University graduate research assistant Zinyang "Ellen" Zhao to provide context, clarity or corrections to spellings of names or dates or to add resources to help readers and researchers to learn about this great man. Additionally, some of the paragraphs or sections were moved to different chapters to help with fluidity of the book, but nothing was omitted that he included. There are a few names or conversations that I could not confirm, but nearly all of the items have been validated through secondary sources or through primary interviews with family members or others.

My hope is that his autobiography will touch you as his life touched me and has influenced me to know myself, to be true to myself, to love my God and family, and to treat others the way I want to be treated.

—Miss Tillery (as Ofield would call me)
Rochelle L. Ford, Ph.D., APR

Dedication

This edited autobiography of Ofield Dukes is dedicated to Roxi Trapp-Dukes Victorian for being Ofield's first mountain top experience, greatest gift and source of inspiration. Secondly, it is dedicated to Michael B. Victorian, who was taught public relations by two of Ofield's mentees and the co-editors of this autobiography, who worked for him as an intern and who represents the thousands whom Ofield mentored and taught. Finally, it is dedicated to Michael Dukes Victorian, Ofield's grandson and son from the union of Roxi and Michael. This grandson represents his third mountain top experience and the future.

Acknowledgements

First, I would like to thank our Lord Jesus Christ for his grace and mercy and allowing me to complete the editing of Ofield Duke's autobiography.

Second, I would like to thank Ofield for believing in me and entrusting me with this project when you knew so many amazing professionals and scholars. I feel blessed to have been your mentee.

Next, I want to acknowledge the Syracuse University S.I. Newhouse School for providing funding for a graduate research assistant and time to complete this project.

Thank you Zinyang "Ellen" Zhao for being a dedicated graduate research assistant. She is a hot ticket on the communications market both here and in China. Check her out! Without her professional, detailed and timely research and formatting, I still would be talking about editing this memoir.

To Shelley Spector, a wonderful Newhouse alumna and founder and president of the Public Relations Museum, thank you for agreeing to publish his autobiography even though it took longer than I had hoped it would take.

And a big thank you and note of appreciation to Dr. Unnia Pettus for being a co-editor on this project, working on it through her illness and encouraging me to get it done.

Note that a portion of the proceeds from the sale of this book will go to the Ofield Dukes Scholarship at Howard University, which was established with funding from Cathy Hughes and friends of Ofield Dukes.

And most of all thank you to Roxi Trapp-Dukes Victorian for trusting me to complete this task of editing her daddy's autobiography and for trusting the Public Relations Museum with some of his most treasured memoires and mementos to be shown at the Museum of Public Relations in New York and with publishing this autobiography.

—Rochelle L. Ford, Ph.D., APR

Foreword

As a Howard University broadcast journalism undergraduate student, I did not have the experience of being taught by Mr. Ofield Dukes in a classroom. However, when I graduated in May 1990, with Summa Cum Laude honors, I was hired to be the deputy press secretary to Reverend Jesse L. Jackson, Sr., founder and president of the National Rainbow Coalition, based in the Washington, D.C. headquarters. Within a month, I was promoted to press secretary, responsible for working closely with the communications director, coordinating the day-to-day media relations duties for this iconic civil rights leader.

In this role, I was formally introduced to Mr. Ofield Dukes when he gave me a congratulatory call regarding my appointment. He offered his assistance in helping me be successful as a recent Howard School of Communications graduate and treated me to our first lunch together. From that lunch in 1990 until his transition from labor to reward in 2011, he's the only person I called my professional mentor. To date, his passing remains one of the greatest losses of my life.

To know Mr. Dukes, is to know his greatest joy and accomplishment was being the father to his only child, Mrs. Roxi Trapp-Dukes Victorian. He would refer to this honor as his first mountain top experience. Becoming the recipient of the Public Relations Society of America's Gold Anvil Award was the greatest joy of his career. He referred to this industry honor as his second mountain top experience. And becoming grandfather to Michael Dukes Victorian—from the union of Roxi and her husband, Mr. Michael B. Victorian brought the third mountain top experience of his life.

This autobiography provides a front-row seat to the life of the most incredible mentor, educator, advisor and strategist the field of public relations will ever know, in my opinion. His reputation was impeccable, because he was a man of faith who overcame great obstacles in life, yet succeeded beyond even his own expectations.

I thank my Lord and Savior, Jesus Christ, for allowing me to share my personal and professional valley highs and mountain lows with Mr. Ofield Dukes in my life. As one of his mentees, he encouraged me to obtain my master's degree and doctorate, as he did with Dr. Rochelle L. Ford, the lead editor of his memoir. And he advised me on every career move, his counsel was priceless. The greatest honor he bestowed me as a practitioner and researcher was allowing me to collaborate with him as an associate. He loved supporting me through retaining my services through my firm, then Pettus & Associates PR, now Pettus PR, LLC, whenever he could. We worked together promoting many annual events, including Bethune Cookman Award Dinners, National Newspaper Publisher Association conferences, Congressional Black Caucus Foundation events and with one of his corporate clients, Pfizer Pharmaceuticals.

While teaching as an adjunct professor, hired by Dr. Barbara Hines, at Howard University in the Department of Journalism, I had the honor of Ofield giving a guest lecture every semester I taught a public relations writing course there. Despite his hectic schedule and global roster of celebrity and corporate clients, and political leaders, he accepted each invitation. My students knew his ethical philosophy, and the importance of education. His love for teaching and mentoring thousands of students was endless.

I would like to thank Dr. Rochelle L. Ford for completing the task of editing his memoir. I'm honored to have been chosen by Roxi and you to be a co-editor because this was the project he wanted to complete more than anything. God allowed him, in his own words, to share his legacy before his health worsened. No one else but you Rochelle, did he ever mention to me, to work with to ensure this autobiography would be edited and shared as he would like.

My deepest thanks to Roxi for entrusting Rochelle and me with your dad's personal memoir. I also thank you, Roxi, for allowing me to fulfill his wish of being a source of spiritual support in your life. It was the hardest task in my ministry to be asked by him to be his "personal pastor" through his health challenge. He never wavered in his faith of being healed and able to watch Michael Dukes Victorian grow up. But as a Christian man, he knew whatever his fate, he would be reunited with you all again.

Now, join us as you read this memoir of the life and legacy of Mr. Ofield Dukes. To God be the glory for the things He has done!

—Reverend Unnia L. Pettus, Ph.D.

In Memory

My father was a man of few words and large actions. He was a change agent, a bridge between a rock and a hard place. My father was a master of relationships with a thoughtfulness and charisma that is unparalleled. He was spirit and light, a giant among giants. He was public relations. While I believe I held his heart, public relations was his passion and truth was his guiding force.

When asked to write this dedication for his autobiography, I was in the midst of reading a book he gave me on Christmas day in 2008, *A Letter to my Daughter*, by Maya Angelou. Oftentimes as I read books that he left in my possession, some with highlights and underlines, I quietly hear the whisper of his sweet tones sharing his most introspective and poignant moments with me, his only daughter.

While my degrees and certificates are not those of a public relations practitioner, the lessons that I learned from my father and the profession are priceless. The importance of knowing thyself and standing firmly in your worth have been invaluable. His diligent work ethic and his mantra in being excellent in everything that you commit to have served both me and my family as we continue to grow in purpose and love.

I sometimes think that my son may truly live in the spirit of my father as I watch him develop. Here is the place where I cry...I remember when my dad was thinking heavily on something in the evening after putting away work for the day, he would make a nice bowl of frozen yogurt or vanilla ice cream, a scoop of peanut butter and watch Sports Center. And though there is no Sport Center in my background, here I sit with a bowl of ice cream and a scoop of peanut butter to ease the pain that still comes from living and conquering without him.

So, my only thoughts to you, the reader of this autobiography, is that you are able to embrace the student inside of you and allow the stories and lessons of his life to resonate and inspire you toward excellence, progress, social justice and change for the betterment of those immediately around you and the world and communities in which you reside.

To the world of public relations, I thank you for the abundance of joy that you brought to my dear father and the lessons and comfort that you can continue to provide.

And to Aunt Unnia, my "Mother Sister" (the character actress Ruby Dee played in Spike Lee's film "Do the Right Thing"), thank you for always watching me, loving me, praying for me and reminding me of my legacy.

Let the pages turn...and let his story be told.

Ashé,
Roxi Trapp-Dukes Victorian, Ofield Dukes'
daughter

Contents

OFIELD DUKES WITH
ROCHELLE L. FORD, PH.D., APR & REV. UNNIA L. PETTUS, PH.D.

**The Autobiography of
Public Relations Man Ofield Dukes**

Ofield

Ofield Dukes
with Rochelle L. Ford, PhD
& Rev. Unnia L. Pettus, PhD

Ofield: The Autobiography of Public Relations
Man Ofield Dukes

By OFIELD DUKES
with ROCHELLE L. FORD, Ph.D., APR
& Rev. UNNIA L. PETTUS, Ph.D.

First edition, 2017
Library of Congress Control Number: 2017951705
ISBN 978-0-9990245-1-5

PUBLISHED BY PRMUSEUM PRESS, LLC, NEW YORK, NEW YORK

I.

An Unexpected Career Impact

It was a typical hot, sultry July day in Washington, D.C. The year was 2001. As I sat in my home office the telephone rang. I was greeted by Kelly Womer, who was calling from the airport in New York City. She had just left a meeting of the Public Relations Society of America's 2001 Individual Awards Committee, which she chaired.

"Mr. Dukes, I have good news for you. You have been named unanimously as recipient of the 2001 PRSA Gold Anvil, the highest award given in the public relations industry."

"Really?" came from my stunned response. There was a long pause as I whispered a silent prayer. "Thank you, Jesus. Thank you, Jesus for this miracle."

I finally said aloud, "I just can't believe it. Really?"

My mind went back to the year 2000 and a letter I received from Ms. Wormer informing me that "The PRSA Honors and Awards Committee was impressed with your long and distinguished public relations career and your services to PRSA. But the letter went on to say that the CEO of one of the largest PR firms in the county had won the award. Her letter also indicated that my name would be held for consideration for 2001. It was sort of bizarre that it really had happened.

After hanging up the phone, I sat there at my desk shaking my head in disbelief, wiping tears from my eyes and saying another prayer of thanks. During 32 years in public relations, I had struggled, worked extra hard, with a passion to be excellent and the best I could be. I wanted to prove that a Colored man, a Negro, a Black, an African American could successfully operate in the mainstream of the public relations industry. Even though the playing field was only somewhat level. I inhaled deeply and again said a silent prayer of thanks for it had been a long, rocky, difficult journey to reach the pinnacle.

As I learned later, I was to be the first person of color in the 50-year existence of the Public Relations Society of America to receive the Gold Anvil award. Looking back, I never could have imagined my career in public relations.

But my story doesn't begin here. My life has been full of many twists and turns—painful encounters with racial discrimination, having to navigate around racial road blocks, detours and bumps and potholes. Some unexpected accomplishments and remarkable experiences also were part of my journey. Let's begin with my family.

II.

The Early Dukes Family

I was born on August 8, 1932 in Rutledge, Alabama, a rural community in Crenshaw County outside the city of Luverne. It is located between Mobile and Montgomery.

My 98-year old aunt Clattie Mae Dukes, who even today maintains a remarkable memory, told me that my parents had lived in a rented one-bedroom house, behind a creek and near a sprawling cotton field.[1] My parents, Violet and Garfield Dukes, made their living as sharecroppers, picking cotton on land owned by whites.

My parents labored hard in the cotton field every day, had the cotton they picked weighed, received some compensation and then paid off their landlord, while raising their own crops of vegetables—peas, corn, tarnish green, cubbish, string beans, white and red potatoes, squash—hogs, chickens and cows, and so forth.

When I was born, my mother was attended by a midwife. It was during the Great Depression, which was the worst of times for whites, but more so for Negroes

---

[1] Clattie Mae Dukes was born in 1913 and died in 2014 at 101 years old.

who were forced to endure the most rigid form of racial discrimination and degradation imaginable.

When I was maybe four of five, I remember my mother carrying me on the edge of her cotton sack because she was using both hands to pick cotton. There were no other babysitting arrangements, no preschool, and no head start. That was the way it was.

When I was six years old, I remember walking with my older sister, Arlene, miles across a creek, through the woods to a segregated one-room school house. It was behind the family church and adjacent to the cemetery. One cold wintry day there was no wood for the pot-bellied stove. The teacher asked students to go out into the cemetery and woods, into the cold, to find twigs and branches so she could build a fire to warm the classroom, so that we could have class.

In 1939, my father left the family to migrate to Detroit where he joined his brother, Greelie Dukes, hoping to land a job in the auto industry. Henry Ford was recruiting Negros from the South for the revolutionary salary of five dollars per day, my father described to me. My father got a job at the Ford Motor Company.

In 1940, my Uncle Greelie Dukes and his wife, Clattie Mae, drove his new Chevrolet to Rutledge to pick up my mother, three sisters and me and take us to join our father in Detroit.

I was blessed with a happy family life. The Dukes family lived in the so-called "Black Bottom" in the rigidly racially segregated city of Detroit.[2] At that time, Negroes were treated as second-class citizens. There were no Negro elected officials in the city government, on the school board, or employed by Wayne County government, and there were no Negroes on Detroit's professional sports teams.

In the 1940's, no Negroes were featured on television, except a Negro wrestler, the Black Panther, who always lost to whites.[3] So, we had no role models or sources of inspiration on television. However, we did have *Amos and Andy* on the radio, a program replete with buffoonery common stereotypes of Colored people.

There were no Negroes employed by retail stores or any other firms or restaurants in white collar positions. And Negroes were not welcomed at downtown restaurants.

---

[2] Originally named "Black Bottom" in the nineteenth century because of the rich soil the French used for farming. Later in the early 1900s during the great migration, the "Black Bottom" became known for being primarily an African American community. The Black Bottom was located northeast of downtown, and sat between Gratiot Avenue, Brush Street, Vernor Highway and the Grand Trunk Railroad tracks. http://roguehaa.com/a-brief-history-of-detroits-black-bottom-neighborhood/

[3] Jim Mitchell wrestled using the name the Black Panther until 1956 when he lost to boxing legend Joe Lewis.

One of the most traumatic experiences of my youth was the race riots in Detroit in 1943.[4] The violence and deaths that ensued created even more tension and fear between the races and led to whites fleeing the city.

From an individual perspective, despite these adverse circumstances of my environment, I was able to maintain my self-esteem and faith in God and in me that one day, maybe one day Colored people will cross over our own River of Jordan to a greater promise land, to a new day of freedom from racial oppression. This was my quiet hope, my constant prayer.

My father, who worked at the Ford Motor Company, later got a job at U.S. Rubber.[5] He attended barber school at night, eventually received his barber's

---

[4] Considered among the worst race riots during the World War II era, this Detroit race riot lasted about 24 hours on June 20 and 21, 1943 and grew out of tensions associated with the increased number of Black migrants from the South seeking factory jobs, yet facing a housing shortage and then moving into new public housing near White neighborhoods. http://www.blackpast.org/aah/detroit-race-riot-1943.

[5] U.S. Robber was originally used in text but editors substituted U.S. Rubber as it was a major employer in Detroit and employed Blacks according to *Rainbow at Midnight: Labor and Culture in the 1940s* by George Lipsitz.
https://books.google.com/books?id=lC9O8kRzinMC&pg=PA77&lpg=PA77&dq=us+rubber+company+detroit+1940+hiring+Blacks&source=bl&ots=AXXc6TeIF6&sig=CX8QWzMUkrEwXURuazqtZci Ysmo&hl=en&sa=X&ved=oahUKEwiLgYzfo7bRAhUC5CYKHYdvA-IQ6AEIGjAA#v=onepage&q=us%20rubber%20company%20detroit%201940%20hiring%20Blacks&f=false

license and opened his own shop on Detroit's East Side. He operated Dukes Barber Shop for more than 40 years until he came disabled.

My dad was a man of a few words at home. When he came home from the barber shop, he would go straight to his favorite chair in the living room. Seated comfortably, he would take out a pad and paper and figure out number combinations to play in the daily numbers game, the lottery of that time. The "numbers man" could knock on our back door the first thing in the morning to collect the two dollars or so my father would play on numbers in the first and second races.[6] Almost all adults in the community played the daily numbers, a form of gambling that was a cultural staple of the ghetto. This gaming exercise was run by prominent Negroes who also gave back to the community. Two of the most successful Negro businessman were the backers of the numbers. Throughout the day, people sitting on their porches or at work, waited with patient excitement for the word on the winning numbers combination for the day. And whenever my dad would "hit" the numbers he would share his winnings with my mother.

My mother, who was short in stature, was a lady of charm and grace who took great pride in her clean house. A devout Christian, she got up every morning with what

---

[6] Numbers were associated both with random drawings and with horse race betting.

she called her "Jesus-given joy" and would not allow anyone to take it from her or tamper with it. She always spent part of her day being in touch with others, neighbors, friends, relatives, offering a word of cheer and inspiration.

My mom enjoyed being a homemaker and cooking regular meals for the family. It was a daily ritual for all of us to have breakfast and dinner together. My mother was not only a great cook; she was a "gourmet" soul food cook. We all loved her yummy T-cakes, delicious banana pudding, sumptuous chocolate cake and sweet potato pie that would melt in your mouth.

The entire Dukes family was undergirded by a strong Christian faith. My sisters Arlene, Lou Alice, Anne, Betty and I looked forward to putting on our "Sunday's best" to go to church with our parents, to worship our Lord and fellowship with our friends. This was our socialization. We had our house, lived in a safe segregated neighborhood, and enjoyed even the limitations of life.

My father served as an usher at church. My mother sang in the choir, as did my sisters Lou and Betty. I was a member of the Church of our Father's Inspiration choir and served as its president. I also taught Sunday school to younger boys.

I learned important principles from my parents. One was the Golden Rule, which meant treating all people with respect as you would want to be treated, trying hard to love all people, without prejudice. I never heard my mother or father utter unkind words about others.

They felt very good about themselves. My dad, although quiet and soft-spoken at home, was very loquacious at his barbershop, engaging his customers on any subject they wanted to discuss. He was a kind-hearted man. And, for whatever reason, I escaped being scolded or reprimanded by my parents for errant behavior.

When I was 11 years of age, I got a job as a *Detroit Times* newspaper carrier, with 90 customers. I delivered daily newspapers for my customers for four years, hardly ever missing a day, despite snowstorms, frigid weather, rain storms, hot and humid days. I developed a young business sense for punctuality, dependability, financial accountability and frugality from this job. My sisters often complained to my mother that her son failed to wash dishes or carry out the garbage. My mother's response was always, "Your brother is busy delivering his newspapers."

In January 1980, we were happy to celebrate the 50th anniversary of our beloved parents. In a newspaper article on the anniversary, my father was quoted as saying that although he worked two jobs to educate his children, he never let his wife work. "She had a full-time job rearing our children."

My sister, Arlene, married Roger Brown, and they became the parents of two girls, Angela and Aleeyce.[7]

Next to me was Lou Alice, who was a star athlete at Miller High School. She married her college boyfriend, Gerald Brock, and they became the parents of two, Rodney and Geraldine. Lou worked at Chrysler Corporation as an administrator of Chrysler Corporation's Vocational Rehabilitation Program until her retirement.

My sister, Anne, was also a high school athlete. She married Alex Harris, of Buffalo, who starred in basketball and football at Virginia Union in Richmond, Virginia. In the Buffalo Public School System, Anne became a reading supervisor, and Alex was a high school guidance counselor. Both retired and took refuse from the bitter, snowy winters of Buffalo for a luxurious winter home in Orlando, Florida.

And my younger sister, Betty Hayden, retired from her job as a personnel management analyst for the Wayne County Department of Human Services.

---

[7] Arlene Brown was a homemaker, worked part-time at Sears teaching sewing and later retired as a sales associate, according to personal correspondence with Roxi Trapp-Dukes Victorian. Roger Brown was an army veteran, worked in multiples roles including building inspector for the city and FAA administrator, and retired from Highland Park School District as the districts building administrator according to personal correspondence with Roxi Trapp-Dukes Victorian.

In May of 1990, my mother had a reoccurrence of cancer, and we celebrated her home going. In the eulogy, the Rev. H. Kearney, pastor of Mt. Calvary Baptist Church, said, "Mrs. Dukes, every day of her life, was the finest example of a Christian who loved her God and in that spirit reached out with genuine love and friendly concern for all those she met." She was 84 and a former *Michigan Chronicle* newspaper "Mother of the Year."

As we, my four sisters and I, were in the funeral limousine traveling from the church to the cemetery to bury our mother, we were mindful of our mother's advice to us not to mourn her home-going. So, we were in the limo listening to a NBA championship basketball game between the Detroit Pistons and the Los Angeles Lakers. When the Pistons won, my sisters cheered, probably puzzling the driver.

Shortly thereafter, in August of 1990, my father passed away, following an extended struggle with Alzheimer's disease. He was 81.

And again, as my sisters and I were in the funeral limo traveling from the church to the cemetery to bury our father, one of my sisters raised the question should anything happen to me in Washington, D.C. who would be there to take care of me.

At first, I ignored the question, and I said, "I don't need any help." My sisters chimed in, together, "Oh yes you do." Added another, "We don't want you to make

another mistake in marriage, as a result of your divorce."
We all laughed.

That was the nature of my family, even during those difficult times in the loss of parents we loved so very, very much. We all had a strong religious perspective and thanked the Good Lord for allowing us to spend so many happy years with our mom and dad.

III.

High School

I attended the only all-Negro high school in the city, Sidney D. Miller High School, just a block on Dubois Street from the family residence. Miller faced the challenges of secondary facilities, resources, and old books. The teachers, however, were first class. They were dedicated and gave us the best education possible.

At Miller, at one point, I had a fleeting fantasy based on the environment in the ghetto, of seeing the persons with fancy cars and well dressed, the numbers man and the pimp. So, my fleeting fantasy was one day "becoming a pimp, a chance taker, easy money maker and the hero to any poor girl's dream."

However, I pursued an aspect of this fantasy by joining the school's newspaper staff and doing a series of romantic stories with a dramatic ending in the style of Eugene O'Neill, a personal favorite of mine at the time.[8]

---

[8] Eugene Gladstone O'Neill (1888–1953) was an American playwright who won the 1936 Nobel Prize for Literature. His dramatic plays were known for tragic realism. http://www.eoneill.com/biography.htm.

One of the life-changing encounters in high school was serving as student manager of Miller's winning basketball team, under Coach Will Robinson, whose philosophy had a tremendous impact on my young life, and I went through a great life's change.

Coach Robinson had a strict, a strong, realistic philosophy for his varsity players:

> There is no substitute for hard work. If you want to be a champion, you have to think like a champion, act like a champion. Although you have two strikes against you, your race and attending a second-class high school, the question is what are you going to do with the third strike? Excuses don't count. You have to work extra hard to overcome your disadvantages and to feel confident in competing against the advantaged. What's critically important is to work extra hard to be excellent and prepare yourself for the opportunity, whenever it comes. We must be prepared for every game, without any excuses, and in life, we have to deal with every adversity with our best ability, without any excuses. There is no substitute for not being excellent, playing and being at your best at all times.

I have remembered those words since. I became an astute student of Coach Robinson's philosophy, and I began to feel like a member of the varsity team. Coach Robinson became my mentor at a crucial stage in my life, a person I admired and respected.

He represented a strong foundation for my future advancement in life.

Coach Robinson's philosophy represented a more positive outlook on life, having a vision beyond the long, dark shadows of the ghetto. He stressed getting a strong education having high self-esteem and self-confidence.

In high school, I developed a deep interest in journalism; learning to write was a struggle. As for my spelling, it was a major problem at the time.

Still, my high school years were memorable. I was very active in extra-curricular activities. I sang in the choir, wrote for the yearbook, served as president of the 12B class and vice president of the senior class.

Upon graduation, at last, in 1950, I attempted to enter Wayne State University in Detroit, but, unfortunately, my grades were so mediocre that I had to take the entrance exam twice. I failed both times. So, my alternative was to take non-matriculating classes in the evening.

Being so young, made it hard to find a job. In seeking work, the only job I could find was one at Sears, Roebuck & Company. I can still remember my interview at Sears, Roebuck & Company. During my interview, I inquired about job opportunities. I was told by a white woman in the interview that Sears did not hire Colored people in sales, in the stock room or at the service station as mechanics. I found out the only job available to people of color was in maintenance as a janitor.

I managed to get hired.

So, for two years, I got up at 5 a.m. to be at Sears at 6 a.m. to join the maintenance team to mop the floors, clean up, and so forth. After the mopping chores, I had the responsibility of outdoor cleanup of the streets surrounding Sears and the parking lot.

This was a difficult period, in a racially segregated city, where all downtown department stores, other retail outlets, the media, daily newspapers, TV stations had a similar racial policy of not hiring Colored people in "white collar" jobs. So, I had no vision and limited hope of escaping Detroit's ghetto, of navigating around the confining racial policies and limitations.

IV.

Induction into the Military

With the country engaged in a military conflict in Korea, at the age of 18, I received my initial notice from Uncle Sam about mandatory registration for military service. Since I was not a full-time college student, I was classified Class A.

On the day that I reached the age of 19, in 1952, I was drafted into the U.S. Army. I remember that particular day of leaving my home to catch the bus for the military recruitment station. I got up at 5 a.m. My mother also got up and prepared breakfast for her only son.

Here's is what I previously wrote about that day:

The alarm clock sounded like an explosion. The time was 4:45 a.m. The date was September 14. The year: 1952. The place 2138 Dubois Street, a residence on Detroit's lower east side. A 19-year-old, who agonized during the night over this moment, struggled out of bed. He had been drafted for active duty in the United States Army, for possible service in the Korean Conflict.

He moved quietly from his bedroom to the bathroom, not wanting to awaken his four sisters, mother and father. But when he emerged from the bathroom, he was not surprised to see his mother warming the skillet for a bacon and eggs and toast breakfast.

The young man dressed quickly, quietly ate his breakfast, hugged his mother at the door and walked across the street toward the bus stop. He turned, paused, looked back at the darkened house, saw his mother looking out the window, then there was a second, third, fourth and fifth face. He waved and headed toward the bus stop.

The young man wondered...would he ever return home? Would he return to a job at Sears, Roebuck & Company as a porter? Accepting a job in maintenance...mopping the floor...taking out trash...sweeping and keeping the parking lots clean? Would life be different, if he returned?

After basic training at Fort Bliss in El Paso, Texas, I was on a military ship headed to Korea. Upon arriving in Korea, I was met by a soldier in a jeep who was to take me to the 2nd Infantry, AAA Battalion. As we were traveling in high speed in the dark of night on a rocky road on the side of a huge mountain, we encountered incoming artillery shells from the enemy. The driver stopped the jeep, and we dashed for cover in a nearby ditch in the dark of night. This was my terrifying greeting in this new strange land of brutal warfare, of inhumanity to mankind.

I spent the first nine months with a six-member team on an anti-aircraft vehicle, overseeing the Chorwon Valley, five miles from the front lines. It was on that hill in Korea, in the lonely dark moments of the night, while on guard duty, four hours on and four hours off, sitting behind a Quad 50 machine gun that I discovered the light of my future being. And it was during those four hours off that a young man was hungry, thirsty for knowledge about himself, about life, about his future.

During this period, I had plenty of time to think, to introspect, to discover who I was, to ponder my future, to decide on a career goal of one day becoming a journalist. And in that connection, I became addicted to words, to expanding my vocabulary. I did a lot of reading and wrote down every word that attracted my attention, then studying the etymology of the word, the diction and usage of the word. I counted about 3,000 words that I had collected, and I prayed that one day I would be able to return 8,000 miles back to America, back to Detroit to pursue my dream of one day becoming a journalist.

I was fortunate to spend the remaining four months in Korea as a writer for the Second Infantry Division newsletter.

In September of 1954, the joyful day of discharge from the U.S. Army came.

V.

Wayne State University

I prepared myself to take the entrance exam at Wayne State University, passed it and began my studies to become a journalist. I was able to finance my way through Wayne using the G.I. Bill, which amounted to $150 per month. My family still was of very moderate means.

While at Wayne, Coach Will Robinson, who also served as the Sports Editor of the Detroit edition of the *Pittsburgh Courier*, had me cover high school sports for the paper. This was my beginning as a cub reporter. After a couple of years and improvement in my spelling, I graduated to covering professional sports, in particular the nationally televised boxing matches at Olympia Stadium. This was during a period when the main sports attraction on television was boxing—the Wednesday night Pabst Blue Ribbon fights from Chicago, the Friday night Gillette Blue Blade fights from Madison Square Garden in New York City. This was a remarkable experience because my coverage of the big fights at the Olympia was featured in the national edition of the *Pittsburgh Courier*. I also covered sandlot baseball, the Detroit Tigers and Lions.

At Wayne, I was able to develop a strong philosophy of life. I read Ralph Waldo Emerson's book of insightful essays, and developed an intellectual intercourse with Williams James and his book on pragmatism. James inspired me to adopt the principle of having a positive attitude, a positive outlook on life, a principle of pragmatism, of pursuing those things in life that are practical. James wrote that one of his greatest discoveries of the 20th Century was that a person's attitude determined how far he or she will go in life.

College Graduation and Racial Barriers

A week before graduation, in June 1958, my journalism advisor, Dr. Sprague Holden, called me into his office. As I entered, his head was down, and when he looked up he said, "Ofield, I think you are as good a writer as the six other fellows in your class. I have been able to find jobs for them at the *Detroit Times*, the *Detroit News* and the *Detroit Free Press*." And there was a pause, and then Dr. Holden added, "However, I don't have any contacts at *Jet* or *Ebony* magazines."

Of course, I was jolted by his comments; the realization of the deep, oppressive roots of racism, but this did not discourage me or shatter my dream of one day becoming a journalist. I recalled Ralph

Waldo Emerson's essay on self-reliance.[9] In that essay, Emerson wrote that it was the genius of Beethoven, Mozart, and Plato of having an unfaltering faith in their ability to deal with adversity and moving on to a high level of excellence. This became my mantra.

I also was inspired by several other Greek philosophers: Socrates, who suggested that the first principle of life is to know thyself; Aristotle, who said, simply, be thyself, and Shakespeare, who wrote, "to thine own self be true."

Socrates' message has had tremendous impact on my life because most often we are introduced to ourselves by others and then go through life needing to be validated by others. A main struggle and effort on my part has been to understand and appreciate who I am, to have high self-esteem, high self-confidence, to fully appreciate and take pride in my own humble existence. In my future teachings at Howard University and The American University, this has been a main emphasis, and it directly related to the point made by Dr. William James about the

---

[9] Ralph Waldo Emerson, "Self-Reliance," Essays: First Series (1841). Retrieved from http://www.emersoncentral.com/selfreliance.htm or https://math.dartmouth.edu/~doyle/docs/self/self.pdf

importance of one's attitude about one's self and others that determines one's future destiny.[10]

Journalism Journey and Black Media

After graduation, in June, 1958, I did freelance articles for the Negro weekly, *The Michigan Chronicle*. In July, I received a call from Frank Seymour, general manager of a radio station newly built by three Negro dentists, headed by Dr. Haley Bell. Mr. Seymour asked if I wanted to be the first news director of the radio station, WCHB, located in Inkster, Michigan, just a few miles west of Detroit. I gladly accepted the job at $50 a week, with no expense account.[11]

As the news director, I was up at 5 a.m. and at the radio station by 6:30 a.m. to prepare hourly newscasts. In the late morning, I would leave the station to cover major news events in Detroit and

---

[10] William James (1842–1910) was an American philosopher, psychologist and physician associated with pragmatist school of thought and being a pioneer in functional psychology. Some of his most famous quotes are available at https://www.goodreads.com/author/quotes/15865.William_James.

[11] In 2002, Cathy Hughes, founder and president of Radio One which owns WCHB in Detroit, renamed the building housing WCHB and two other Detroit stations in honor of Ofield Dukes. In 2002 Hughes named the building that would house three of her Detroit stations the Ofield Dukes Communications Center.

then rush back to prepare news and taped interviews for the afternoon newscasts.

In 1960, I had the great pleasure of covering the campaign visit to Michigan of Democratic Presidential Candidate John Fitzgerald Kennedy. And I have a photo of that momentous event.

In 1961, I left the position of news director at WCHB to become a senior editor at the *Michigan Chronicle*, Detroit's main Negro newspapers. Mr. Longworth M. Quinn, the general manager, became my boss and wonderful friend and supporter. There, I covered front-page news, did features, did three original editorials every week, a political column, and "for kicks" a record review column. On the day of deadline, I would sit at my desk, in front of my Underwood typewriter, from 9 a.m. to 5 p.m., having a hot dog or hamburger, writing story after story. This was a great learning experience for me. This is how I had become a writer.

VI.

Young Adult Division of NAACP—Leadership Challenges

During this period, in 1961, I was encouraged to become founder/president of the Young Adult Division of the Detroit NAACP. We became an organization of 150 "militant" professional young adults, teachers, attorneys, business persons, secretaries, among others that became very active in promoting civil and equal rights for Negroes in Detroit.[12] We were well organized into working committees, jobs, housing, education, grassroots politics, mobilization of welfare mothers, among others.

---

[12] *The Crisis* magazine 1962 called the involvement of this new Young Adult Division of the Detroit NAACP in the Campaign to End Job Bias as "a militant and energetic campaign"…"with encouraging success to the major media outlets in Detroit." "What The Branches are Doing," *The Crisis* 69, No. 10 (1962): 616–617. Retrieved on January 11, 2017 from https://books.google.com/books?id=-FsEAAAAMBAJ&lpg=PA616&ots=_EmS36hxbb&dq=Young%20 Adult%20Division%20of%20the%20Detroit%20NAACP%20mi litant&pg=PA573#v=onepage&q=Young%20Adult%20Division% 20of%20the%20Detroit%20NAACP%20militant&f=false.

As the head of the job opportunity committee, I led the effort to meet with the regional president of Sears, Roebuck & Company and negotiated the hiring of the first Negro salesperson, Albert "Al" Dotson, in the vacuum cleaner department.[13] Our Young Adult Division of the Detroit NAACP demonstrated against downtown department's stores and for fair housing. We organized welfare mothers in the Brewster Douglass projects into an active, high influential political force. In politics, we were active in helping to elect the first Negro, Attorney William T. Patrick, Jr., to the City of Detroit Common Council. In addition, we competed with the United Auto Workers (UAW) and religious leaders in fundraising for the Detroit Branch of the NAACP. I was assisted, in particular by a brilliant, highly efficient and dedicated vice president, Sonia Porter, a remarkable person.

---

[13] Albert E. Dotson later became Sear's first Black manager and he also later served as the chairman of the board of trustees for Florida International University in Miami. https://news.fiu.edu/2011/12/former-fiu-board-of-trustee-leader-named-chairman-emeritus/34253 and https://editorialqueen.wordpress.com/2012/12/19/albert-e-dotson-sr-never-settled-for-mediocrity/. His son, Albert E. Dotson, Jr., became the president of One Hundred Black Men and served from 2004–2013, and credits his father for instilling a spirit of activism through his racial barrier breaking career. http://www.thehistorymakers.com/biography/albert-dotson-jr.

1963 March on Washington

A highlight of 1963, was the NAACP bus ride to Washington, D.C. for the 1963 March on Washington, covering the event as a reporter for the *Michigan Chronicle* and WCHB radio. At the march, I had the unique, thrilling experience and surprising privilege of sitting on the steps of the Lincoln Memorial, next to Harry Belafonte, Sidney Poitier and Lena Horne, and others. That was my first significant exposure to Dr. Martin Luther King, Jr. and Washington, D.C. That indeed was a historic moment in my young life.

The evolution of the 1963 March on Washington was a source of intrigue to me, because Louis Martin, a co-founder of the *Michigan Chronicle* and a person who influenced me to come to Washington, indirectly contributed to the civil rights leaders' convening the march.

In an article that I subsequently did on Martin, I reported that during the 1960 presidential campaign, R. Sargent Shriver enlisted Martin to work for the election of his brother-in-law, John F. Kennedy. A few weeks before the November election, Martin reportedly convinced Robert Kennedy, who was running his brother's campaign, to call Judge Oscar Mitchell and persuade him to release Dr. Martin Luther King, Jr. from an Atlanta jail. Dr. King, who had been arrested for joining students during a sit-in at a segregated shop, was freed a day later. Unconfirmed reports indicated that Dr. King would be willing to support the Kennedy candidacy if Mr. Kennedy, once elected, would end discrimination in housing with the stroke of a pen, by executive order.

Politically savvy Martin printed thousands of flyers that were distributed during the presidential campaign on how the Kennedys freed Dr. King from jail, implying King's support for Kennedy's candidacy.

A. Philip Randolph—Elder Statesman of the Civil Rights Movement

As the story goes, President Kennedy was slow about keeping his promise. Somewhat annoyed and concerned about President Kennedy's not moving on civil rights, civil rights leaders met in 1963 to discuss a counter strategy to focus on civil rights. Rev. Walter Fauntroy, of Washington, D.C., and an aide to Dr. King, recalls that meeting being held on July 2, 1963.

Prominent in that meeting were A. Philip Randolph, founder of the Brotherhood of Sleeping Car Porters; his aide, Bayard Rustin; Roy Wilkins, executive of the NAACP; Whitney Young, executive

director of the National Urban League; Dr. Martin
Luther King, Jr., of the Southern Christian
Leadership Conference (SCLC); John Lewis, of the
Student Non-Violent Coordinating Committee; and
James Farmer, of the Congress of Racial Equality. It
was there that a decision was made to host the
March on Washington.

Rep. John Lewis, then a top official of the
Student Nonviolent Coordinating Committee, wrote
in his book, *Walking with the Wind,* about the "Big
Six" civil rights leaders in June of 1963 meeting with
President Kennedy at the White House.

Lewis wrote that President Kennedy was
concerned about violence and the planned March on
Washington. Lewis wrote that "A. Philip Randolph
announced to the President that there would be a
march, the only questions were what form it would
take and those questions, Randolph made clear,
politely, respectfully, but firmly, would be answered
by us, not the government."

Lewis wrote that Dr. Martin Luther King, Jr.
did not speak until the end of the two-hour
meeting—but all deferred to Mr. Randolph "because
he was the dean."

Lewis added that "Although Randolph was
getting up in age, the man still has so much dignity
and pride. He was impressive. Such a wonderful
human being with so much learning, so much grace."

Lewis also wrote that Roy Wilkins, executive director of the NAACP, told President Kennedy that he would have problems with his own organization and membership if they did not have the march. This was evidence that the Kennedy White House was opposed to such a march, fearing some type of violent outbreak.

Rev. Fauntroy added how forceful and impressive Mr. Randolph was in that meeting with President Kennedy. Although Mr. Randolph, with his rich, baritone voice and eloquent oratorical style, could have given a powerful speech at that historic Washington march, it was probably part of his character and humility to suggest that Dr. King be the keynote speaker.

If there is an unsung hero of the civil rights movement, it is A. Philip Randolph. This is the man who built the Brotherhood of Sleeping Car Porters, started the civil rights movement in the 1950's, leading a 1957 prayer-pilgrimage for civil rights and marches for school integration in 1958–59. It was Mr. Randolph who put pressure on and persuaded President Harry S. Truman to end racial discrimination in the military.

Dr. King, rightfully so, received international fame for his courageous leadership in the face of southern violence, but A. Philip Randolph spent many of his years laying the leadership foundation for Dr. King and other civil rights leaders of the 1960s.

So, on that day on August 28, 1963, hundreds of thousands gathered on the mall in front of the Lincoln Memorial. And there was not any official representation from the Kennedy White House. At this particular time, the mainstream media was most protective of the image of the Kennedys, John and Bob, in the White House. The huge, historic march was peaceful. There were no acts of violence anywhere.

VII.

Transition from Detroit to Washington, D.C.

In 1964, at the *Michigan Chronicle*, I won three writing awards of the National Newspapers Publishers Association for editorial, feature and column writing. My work with the *Michigan Chronicle* had attracted the attention of Atty. Hobart Taylor, Jr., a former assistant prosecutor in Detroit and an advisor to President Lyndon B. Johnson at the White House.[14]

Mr. Taylor was in touch with me in January of 1964 about coming to Washington to work in the Johnson-Humphrey administration. Mr. Taylor was quite upset at the time about a pending *Ebony Magazine* article on his being a millionaire. Mr. Taylor wanted me to come to Washington to help protect his image from such allegations. At the time, his father, Hobart Taylor, Sr. was a prominent multi-millionaire in Houston and was active in support of

---

[14] Details about Hobart Taylor, Jr. can be found at http://www.blackpast.org/aah/taylor-hobart-jr-1920-1981.

local civil rights and political activities.[15] Instead of accepting the position, I ended up writing a front-page article for the *Michigan Chronicle*, under a main, bold-faced headline: "NO MILLIONAIRE—Spikes Nation-Wide Rumors—Taylor denies reports."

I must admit my casual response to Mr. Taylor's invitation was because I was satisfied with my $75 a week job at the *Michigan Chronicle* and my female companions. Mr. Taylor, however, was persistent in working on a job situation for me in Washington, and called me in February to keep me informed. In calling on the first of March, he indicated that he had worked out a position for me to be deputy director of public affairs for the President's Committee on Equal Opportunity, at a salary of $10,000 a year. This was double my salary at the *Michigan Chronicle*, but I was still not excited about leaving Detroit.

When two weeks passed, and he did not hear from me, Taylor called Louis Martin, a founder of the *Michigan Chronicle* and advisor to President Johnson as vice chairman of the Democratic National Committee. Mr. Taylor informed him of his efforts to get me to Washington. Mr. Martin promptly called Mr. Quinn, my boss at the *Michigan*

---

[15] Details about Hobart Taylor, Sr. can be found at https://tshaonline.org/handbook/online/articles/fta30.

Chronicle, and advised him to fire me, if necessary, to get me to accept the position in Washington.

I remember the day that Mr. Quinn slowly walked to my desk...and said, "Ofield, the boss, Louis Martin has called.[16] He and Hobart Taylor want you in Washington. And I have been instructed to fire you, if necessary, to get you there." And then Mr. Quinn turned away and went back to his office.

In the first week of April 1964, I loaded a few belongings in my Chevrolet and began the drive to Washington, D.C. My intention was to spend one year in working in Washington and return to dear ol' Detroit.

When I arrived, Taylor and his wife, Lynette, were happy to see me. Taylor had arranged for housing at the same luxury apartment complex where he lived in Southwest Washington. I must say Hobart Taylor, Jr. was most aggressive in getting me to come to Washington, and I will be forever grateful to him for the significant change in my life and my professional destiny.

---

[16] Ofield and others pronounced his name as "Louie" although in this text, Louis is used instead of "Louie."

Job Challenge in Washington, D.C.

Although Hobart Taylor, Jr. was excited about my coming to Washington for a job with the President Committee on Equal Opportunity, Mack Wise, the director of communication for the committee, had his concerns.

Prior to my arrival, Wise wrote the following memo to Taylor:

> I personally would prefer not to hire Odell (misspelling of my first name). He's going to come in with too much of a personal relationship with you and is going to create another problem for me. I know from the way that he writes and from the way that you already talk—but how you've asked to borrow him—that he's going to be running things. And he will feel a certain kinship to you because of these circumstances that will make it difficult for me to deal with. I am dead sure of that. Please, dear God, I don't want any more god dam personnel problems.

There are always a few bumps in the road and the challenge is navigating around them without breaking stride.

In spite of Wise's concerns, Hobart and I maintained a special relationship as African Americans, and it was an adjustment that Mack Wise, a white who wanted to be in control, had to make. And in time, I worked hard, did an effective job as Wise's deputy and was supportive of him. As a result, he and I developed a positive and mutually respective professional relationship.

Early Friendships in Washington, D.C.

I was told that one of my first visits in Washington, D.C. should be the office of Simeon Booker, Washington, D.C. Bureau Chief of *Jet* and *Ebony* magazines. I was fortunate to be warmly greeted by Mr. Booker who became a consistent supporter and genuine friend. He was generous in his coverage of my activities in *Jet* and *Ebony* magazines.

Three friends of Hobart Taylor, Jr.—Ruthie Leffall, Valerie Pinson, and Pat Seldom—were quick to adopt me as a friend and, to my surprise, hosted a birthday party for me in August of 1964.

Many Faces of Washington, D.C.

Washington, D.C., the nation's capital, is a national and world-wide tourist attraction for its historic monuments, for its beauty, for its grandeur, and its aura of excitement. The city is captivating, a tremendous source of American history. It is the political heart of America, with the weekly deliberations of members of Congress, and the periodic sessions of the Supreme Court.

With so many public relations, public affairs, information, and communications professionals and lobbyists, Washington is the public relations capital of the world. Nothing happens in the city without a mixture of public relations and politics.

Thousands of people, many college graduates, migrate to Washington to advance their careers. There are many levels to Washington, depending on where you work and live. Relationships are developments at these levels.

On a community basis, Washington is disconnected. People are disconnected geographically based on which of the eight wards they live in and the name of the area. I lived in Southwest. Other D.C. residents live in Foggy Bottom, Georgetown, Friendship Heights, Capitol Hill, Adams Morgan, Trinidad, the Gold Coast, among others. These different areas are represented by Advisory Neighborhood Commission members and neighborhood associations, but lacking is a sense of community and ongoing communication among neighbors. There is a sense of isolation.

At a recent event, the comment was made, if you want a friend in Washington, get a dog. The comment has some implications. Many in Washington develop relationships, not friendships, based on what others can do for them in their career goals. So, these people fall in the category of "acquaintances" and are not necessarily genuine friends interested in your welfare. Very seldom will the question be asked, "Hey, what can I do for you?"

The city has segments of racial segregation. President Lyndon Johnson often spoke of the ugly face of Washington, where there is one of the highest poverty levels in the country—and that is predominantly Black Anacostia or Ward Eight, across the Potomac River from "mainland" District of Columbia.

Across town—in Georgetown and Ward Three in the northwest part of the District—these areas are 99 percent white. In a northern part of the District, called the Gold Coast, live the upper-income African Americans. And the area called Adams Morgan is predominantly Hispanic.

However, racial integration has come to what once was the heart and soul of the so-called "Chocolate City," U Street. Now in 2011, there are as many young white professionals living in the area and strolling the street shopping and walking their pets. Now, there are more Ethiopian restaurants on U Street than Black-owned restaurants.[17] A large percentage of upper and middle-income Blacks have

---

[17] Owned by African American/Black Americans, meaning descendent of slaves, and not recent immigrants of Ethiopia who some might consider to be Black.

moved to Prince George's County (Maryland), which has the largest jurisdiction of upper and middle-income Blacks in the country. *The Washington Post* columnist Courtland Milloy recently described the transformation of the "Chocolate City" to "vanilla swirl."[18]

A challenge for the present Mayor, as well as for former mayors of the District, is somehow developing a sense of unity, a sense of *esprit de corps*. The geographical disconnectedness poses a tremendous challenge.[19]

But there is the contagious Washington "fever" that grabs and absorbs you, especially if you are an astute student and practitioner of the politics of the nation's capital. I love being here.

---

[18] Courtland Milloy, "Bittersweet memories of 'Chocolate City,'" *The Washington Post*, April 19, 2011. Retrieved from https://www.washingtonpost.com/local/bittersweet-memories-of-chocolate-city/2011/04/19/AFrouJ8D_story.html?utm_term=.4c1d8a022ba5.

[19] During the last years of Ofield Dukes' life, Adrian Fenty served as the mayor of Washington, D.C. from 2007–2011, followed by Vincent Gray who served from 2011–2015 when Ofield last edited this memoir on April 15, 2011.

VIII.

First Job in Washington, D.C.— President's Committee on Equal Employment Opportunity

President Lyndon B. Johnson and Civil Rights

As I indicated, my initial job in Washington, D.C. in April of 1964 was at the U.S. Department of Labor, serving as Deputy Director of Public Affairs of the President's Committee on Equal Employment Opportunity. The committee was actively chaired by President John F. Kennedy established the President's Committee on Equal Employment Opportunity in 1961 in partnership with the Plans for Progress program by having companies to submit plans for the voluntary promotion of equal employment opportunities for African Americans. The Plans for Progress program became an important vehicle for Fortune 500 companies to voluntarily promote equal employment by submitting plans for achieving such goals. This was a major brainchild of President Kennedy.

I served in a dual role as deputy director of the President's Committee on Equal Employment Opportunity and director of public affairs for the Plans for Progress program.

In a meeting with company executives in the Indian Treaty Room of the Executive Office Building on May 12, 1964, President Johnson reported 86 companies had submitted their Plans for Progress between January 1961 and January 1963 and increased by 258,853 persons, and that 23.1 percent of those increased employees' jobs went to minority groups.

President Johnson reported at that meeting he had traveled thousands of miles, through 13 states in promoting voluntary equal employment opportunity. This was only an early indication of his intense—and I use the word intense, advisedly—commitment to civil rights and expanding opportunities for African Americans.

Hobart Taylor, Jr. and Labor Secretary W. Willard Wirtz served as co-chairpersons of the President's Committee.[20] G. William Miller,

---

[20] Hobart Taylor, Jr. held the official title of executive vice chairman, and Labor Secretary W. Willard Wirtz held the official title of vice chairman of the President's Committee. Lyndon B. Johnson, "Remarks to the Members of the President's Committee on Equal Employment Opportunity Upon Receiving Their Report," *Public Papers of the Presidents of the United States: Lyndon B. Johnson*, 1963–1964 (Washington, D.C.: Government Printing

president of Textron, Inc., was the effective
president of Plans for Progress.

The year 1964 was a very busy period for
President Johnson, especially in pushing legislation,
Title VII, to end discrimination based on race.[21] The
President hosted a series of national and regional
conferences and special meetings with labor and
business leaders.

I recall an urgently important meeting in the
summer of 1964 President Johnson had in the East
Room of the White House with about 70 chief
executives of major corporations to solicit their
support for the pending Title VII legislation. I stood
in a corner of the East Room as President Johnson
began addressing the group. He began in his folksy
way by saying to the business executives that as their
president, he was there to respond to their needs and
wishes.

Office, 1964), pp. 844–845. Retrieved from
https://books.google.com/books?id=A5_aAwAAQBAJ&pg=PA846
&lpg=PA846&dq=Hobart+Taylor,+Jr.+and+Labor+Secretary+W.+
Willard+Wirtz+served+as+chair+of+the+President%E2%80%99s+
Committee&source=bl&ots=YjxHoGlpIp&sig=_eVtrdHCmBEr6
NhwdgooyicoRXw&hl=en&sa=X&ved=0ahUKEwjmnd-
6_dbRAhUE44MKHU6KAjEQ6AEIGjAA#v=onepage&q=Hoba
rt%20Taylor%2C%20Jr.%20and%20Labor%20Secretary%20W.
%20Willard%20Wirtz%20served%20as%20chair%20of%20the
%20President%E2%80%99s%20Committee&f=false

[21] The Title VII legislation was signed into law in 1964, but the
EEOC officially opened in July 1965.

He asked, "What do you want of me? Do you need tax breaks? Oil depletion allowances? Just tell me what you want to boost the economy, to support the success of your businesses."

The discussion went on for about 30 minutes. As President Johnson was about to leave, moving from the podium, his attention suddenly focused on Hobart Taylor, Jr. standing in the rear of the room. President Johnson returned to the podium and said:

> All of you know Hobart Taylor, who has been working very closely with you through the Plans for Progress program. He is a person of a different color but there are many other Hobart Taylors out there who are interested in being tax payers instead of tax eaters. If given a chance, an equal opportunity, these people can enter the work force and help boost our economy. I have introduced a simple piece of legislation to provide an equal opportunity for them to do this through Title VII. And all I ask of you as your president, who is willing to do those things you have asked of me, I just want you to walk an extra mile with me by supporting Title VII.

President Johnson's persuasive skills carried the day, and he did receive the backing of the business community for Title VII.

However, there were other legislative challenges. A southern senator introduced a resolution designed to sabotage the legislation by adding an amendment to ban discrimination based on sex.

A politically savvy President Johnson wasted no time in responding. He had White House aide Elizabeth Carpenter to convene a press conference at the National Press Club with a roundup of women holding top positions in the federal government.[22] At this press conference, President Johnson announced that he was initiating a movement to free women from employment discrimination by supporting an amendment prohibiting discrimination based on race and sex.

Another tough challenge for President Johnson was gaining support of moderate Republican senators. So, he needed the leadership support of Republican Minority Leader Senator Everett "Ev" Dirksen, Republican of Illinois.

I have many anecdotes involving President Johnson. This one has him calling Senator Dirksen, first speaking to his wife, and then asking to say a word to her husband. President Johnson reportedly said to Senator Dirksen that he commended his being a great fan of President Abraham Lincoln for being the Great Emancipator in freeing the slaves.

---

[22] Also known as Mary Elizabeth or Liz Carpenter. She served as Vice President Lyndon B. Johnson's executive assistant and Lady Bird Johnson's press secretary and staff director.

President Johnson reportedly went on to say to Senator Dirksen that he thought Dirksen was such a great person that he wanted to do what he could to have Dirksen's face etched beside Lincoln's on Mount Rushmore. Before hanging up, President Johnson reminded Senator Dirksen that there was some unfinished work that President Lincoln would have attended to if he were able. That was to free American Negroes from discrimination in employment. Johnson said his Title VII bill would do that and he needed the leadership help of Senator Dirksen to achieve this goal. Johnson got what he wanted...Senator Dirksen responded positively.

With Vice President Hubert H. Humphrey working out of his Capitol Hill office, day and night, coordinating support for the bill, Title VII was eventually passed, with the support of moderate Republicans. Thanks to Senator Dirksen.

Later when AT&T was a public relations client of mine in the 1970s, its Washington director of Public Relations, Charles Dynes, Jr., came to my office to ask my advice on how AT&T should handle a class-action law suit filed by the white switchboard operators at AT&T with the Equal Employment Opportunity Commission, charging the company with wide spread job discrimination based on sex.

My advice to Mr. Dynes was to negotiate a settlement. However, the attorneys for AT&T

refused to settle and pressed ahead. This sent U.S.
Attorney General John Mitchell into a hot rage,
resulting in a front-page article on Attorney General
Mitchell declaring war on AT&T. The white
switchboard operators at AT&T won their class
action lawsuit.

A second class-action lawsuit was filed by white
flight attendants at TWA Airlines. And, they too,
won their case.

Although the legislation was passed in 1964,
statistics in 2011 indicate that white women have
benefited more from Title VII than African
Americans and other minorities. President Johnson,
in fact, became the employment emancipator of
white women, of which he has yet to receive any
credit.

White House National Conference "To Fulfill These Rights"

In 1965, President Johnson announced the
convening in 1966 of a White House National
Conference "To Fulfill These Rights," bringing
together business, labor, civil rights leaders, elected
officials, and representatives of social, civic and
professional groups to discuss the President's priority
agenda for advancing the civil rights of American
Negroes.

One of the people very much involved in shaping the program agenda for the conference was M. Carl Holman, who later became president of the National Urban Coalition. Holman, one of the unsung heroes of the civil rights movement, was a brilliant strategist and had the uncanny ability, the genuine humility of working with all personalities.

Holman began his civil rights involvement in Atlanta as editor of the *Atlanta Inquirer*. As the president of the National Urban Coalition, he was a co-convener with Rep. Walter Fauntroy of strategy sessions with Black elected officials and a cross-section of leaders as part of the annual conference of the Congressional Black Caucus. Holman was a ready resource for all in the civil rights movement. For years, he and I played tennis together. And it was a sacrilege to miss a scheduled tennis engagement with him, or to be late.

In the planning of the White House conference "To Fulfill These Rights," held on June 1 and 2 in 1996, President Johnson had a concern about the lack of communication among the main civil rights leaders, the "Big Six." So, he arranged for a railroad executive from Chicago, Ben W. Heineman, to serve as chairman of the conference and convene briefing meetings in the Indian Treaty Room of the Executive Office Building for civil rights leaders.

I recall how those meetings went. On one side of the room were Roy Wilkins, executive director of the NAACP; Whitney Young, executive director of the National Urban League; A. Philip Randolph, of the Brotherhood of Sleeping Car Porters; and James Farmer, executive director of the Congress of Racial Equality. On the other side of the room were Dr. Martin Luther King, Jr., Rev. Ralph Abernathy, Rev. Andrew Young, and Rev. Walter Fauntroy of the SCLC, and John Lewis, of the Student Non-Violent Coordinating Committee. And in the middle of the room were Dr. Dorothy Height, president of the National Council of Negro Women, and Bayard Rustin, civil rights strategist and aide to A. Philip Randolph.

There obviously existed some tension between the "civil rights established leaders" and the new generation of civil rights activists led by Dr. King— and the great media attention and coverage that Dr. King and his SCLC lieutenants were getting.

After the conference, I was pleased to receive a personal letter from Mr. Heineman, saying "I wish to personally thank you for your excellent support and unselfish efforts as a senior conference staff assistant. Your efforts contributed materially toward the success of the conference."

Heineman's unselfish leadership efforts, at behest of President Johnson, improved a level of communication, cooperation and support of civil rights leaders for the conference.

Another thank you note that I will cherish came from A. Philip Randolph, the honorary chairman of the conference. He wrote:

> Dear Mr. Dukes, I want to express my personal congratulation and appreciation to you for the dedicated, competent, and impressive job you did in helping to mold the epoch-making and tremendously significant White House conference 'To Fulfill These Rights,' called by our great President Lyndon B. Johnson. Let me assure you that it was a great pleasure and honor to have been associated with you in this enriching and rewarding experience, the effect of which was to achieve the dignity of the personality of Colored Americans in particular and all Americans in general. A. Philip Randolph.

And the letter carries his personal signature.

Abolishment of The President's Committee on Equal Employment Opportunity and Implementation of New Law, Title VII

After the passage of the new historic civil rights law, Title VII, banning discrimination based on race and sex, the President's Committee on Equal Employment Opportunity was abolished. I was assigned to the staff of the newly established Equal Employment Opportunity Commission (EEOC), with the responsibility of implementing the anti-job bias provisions of Title VII.

Unexpectedly, I encountered my own job challenge. EEOC Chairman Franklin D. Roosevelt, Jr. brought in, as director of public affairs, a white official from the Peace Corps who decided to bring with him two of his colleagues. Although I had more experience in civil rights and worked with the President's Committee, I became the low-person on the totem pole in public affairs. I wrote a letter of complaint to Mr. Roosevelt, raising questions about the process and fairness. That was a disturbing paradox, feeling some sense of job discrimination at the EEOC. The matter was never resolved, but you accept these challenges, never losing faith in your ability to deal with these bumps in the road, navigate around them without losing your cool, and move on to higher grounds.

At the EEOC, I assumed a responsibility of writing speeches for EEOC member, Samuel C. Jackson, a moderate Black Republican. I also assisted him in making important political contacts with Democrats and others.

IX.

Black Leadership

History-Making Influence of Two Black Men in Washington

I was able to witness the historic political influence of two Black men: Hobart Taylor, Jr., as Associate General Counsel to President Johnson, and Louis Martin, Deputy Chairman of the Democratic National Committee and advisor to President Johnson.

Martin also was a part of the political inner circle of President John Kennedy and a personal advisor. Later, he became a White House advisor to President Jimmy Carter, providing him the unique position in history of being an influential advisor to three American presidents. Martin was respected by all as the epitome of political wisdom, a low-key man of political savvy and great knowledge. After receiving a journalism degree from the University of Michigan, he came to Detroit and was a co-founder of *The Michigan Chronicle*.

Noted Washington syndicated columnist, the late David S. Broder, wrote in a December 24, 1968 column on Martin: "One of the most remarkable, unpublicized success stories of the last eight years is coming to a close with the retirement early next month of Louis Martin, as deputy chairman of the Democratic National Committee. He has moved quietly among the power centers of Washington, promoting the interests of civil rights, Negroes and the Democratic Party and insisting that the three are inextricably linked."[23]

Taylor, a law graduate of the University of Michigan, was an assistant Wayne County Prosecutor before joining the staff of Vice President Johnson in 1961. His father, Hobart Taylor, Sr., a multimillionaire businessman in Houston, Texas, was an early supporter of Johnson's congressional career. The father received a promise from Mr. Johnson that he would take care of his son in Washington.

Taylor, Jr., too, was a brilliant legal mind, sharp political thinker, with a keen business sense and impeccable judgment. He was unique in his close and accepted relations with Fortune 500 business executives. At the Johnson White House, Taylor was on par with the rest of the staff. He was also an indispensable advisor to President Johnson.

---

[23] David S. Broder, "Little-Known Party Official Pressed Gains for Negroes," *The Washington Post*, December 24, 1968, p. 37. Retrieved from Proquest.com.

On one politically sensitive occasion, there was a conflict between Secretary of Labor Willard Wirtz and Taylor, Jr. over who had top authority in the decision-making process of the President's Committee on Equal Employment Opportunity and Plans for Progress. President Johnson resolved the problem by moving Taylor's office from the Department of Labor to the White House as associate general counsel.

These two political stalwarts made history by being two of the most influential players in the high stakes of politics in the nation's capital. It is unfortunate that very little will be written about them in history books, because they learned the important art of Washington politics, of working behind the scenes. I was most fortunate to have Louis Martin and Hobart Taylor, Jr. as my mentors and loyal friends who helped me make early adjustments to a new world of Washington, D.C. They both made a big difference in my Washington advancement and eventful care.

Two Black Women of Tremendous Influence on Capitol Hill

It is unlikely that that any history books or pamphlets on the Black political empowerment movement that swept our nation's capital in the

1960s will mention the names of two women who packed a lot of political power in their positions in the U.S. Congress.

Mrs. Christian Davis was chief of staff for Rep. William Dawson, of Chicago, as the first Black chairman of the Government Operations Committee, overseeing the budgets of several federal agencies.[24] And Louise Maxienne Dargans was chief clerk for the House Education and Labor Committee, chaired by the very powerful Rep. Adam Clayton Powell, of New York.[25] President Johnson worked hand-in-glove with Rep. Powell to produce a minimum wage bill and other education legislation as part of his "Great Society" programs. Dawson and Powell were both Democrats while in Congress.

Mrs. Davis and Mrs. Dargans were strong women who knew the inter-operations of the House of Representatives and used the power of their offices intelligently and effectively. They were,

---

[24] Dukes pronounced her name Christian, but according to Christine R. Davis http://dh.howard.edu/cgi/viewcontent.cgi?article=1053&context=fi naid_manu, her name was spelled Christine R. Davis.

[25] Maxienne, as Ofield called her, also served as research director for the Labor Committee in 1974 according to *Ebony* magazine, after 30 years working on Capitol Hill, beginning as an administrative assistant to Adam Clayton Powell in 1945. "Black Women on Capitol Hill," *Ebony*, June 1974, p. 122.

indeed, Black women of great political influence and used it authoritatively.

Appointment of Thurgood Marshall to U.S. Supreme Court

An example of the background influence of Black advisors to President Johnson was his decision to appoint Thurgood Marshall as Solicitor General and to the Supreme Court. Louis Martin and Hobart Taylor, Jr. were among those who urged the President to make such a historic move.

At the White House ceremony for Mr. Marshall as a new member of the high court, President Johnson looked out over the audience and he did not see Louis Martin who helped him make such a decision. President Johnson held up the ceremony. He had the White House switchboard operator find Martin. Martin was on the golf course enjoying his favorite pastime. President Johnson ordered him to the White House for the Marshall ceremony. That indicated the political significance of a Black man who made history by being a personal advisor to three U.S. presidents, John F. Kennedy, Lyndon B. Johnson and Jimmy Carter. Louis Martin was considered a political genius. I was fortunate to have the experience of being his protégé and working closely with him.

Black Editors and Publishers, President Johnson—More Negro Generals

Louis Martin, as vice chairman of the Democratic National Committee and as a personal advisor to President Johnson, and I would arrange for a group of Black editors and publishers, representing the National Newspaper Publishers Association (NNPA), to come to Washington sometimes twice a year, in the spring and fall, to meet with Vice President Humphrey and President Johnson.

In 1966, the NNPA publishers met with the President at the White House. Dr. Carlton Goodlett, publisher of the *San Francisco Sun Reporter*, raised the question with President Johnson about the only two Negro generals being a part of the Davis family.[26] Dr. Goodlett wanted to know why there were not more Negro generals. President Johnson said the question should be raised with Secretary of Defense Robert McNamara and the Joint Chiefs of Staff. Mr. Johnson said he would arrange for the

---

[26] Benjamin O. Davis, Sr. was the first Negro general in the U.S. Army and his son Benjamin O. Davis, Jr. was the first Negro general in the U.S. Air Force and the second Negro general in the U.S. military. "Benjamin O. Davis, Jr., First Negro General," *The New York Times*, November 27, 1970, p. 1. Retrieved from http://www.nytimes.com/1970/11/27/archives/benjamin-davis-sr-first-negro-general-in-us-dies-at-93-benjamin-o.html

publishers to meet with Secretary McNamara and the Joint Chiefs of Staff the next day.

I attended the meeting in Secretary McNamara's conference room, also attended by the top brass of the military. I have photos of that occasion. During the meeting, Dr. Goodlett, PhD, MD, and most scholarly and articulate, stood up and introduced himself. He told Secretary McNamara that he, too, was a graduate of the University of California at Berkeley. He challenged the military establishment on the fact that the only two Negro generals were Gen. Benjamin Davis and his son.

Dr. Goodlett raised the pointed question, "Secretary McNamara, do you think we as Negroes should wait until the Davis family engaged in fancy inter-breeding before we can have a third Negro general?'

Secretary McNamara almost fell out of his chair in his surprise at such a question. However, he did recover and promised Dr. Goodlett and the NNPA editors and publishers that he would set in motion an affirmative action program to increase top opportunities for minorities in the military. One of the eventual products of that affirmative action program was General Colin Powell and dozens of other Negro generals in the military.

President Johnson and the Fight for the Fair Housing Law of 1968

In 1968, Louis Martin and I arranged for the NNPA publishers to meet with President Johnson in March of that year at the White House.[27] This turned out to be a very busy day for President Johnson in meetings with his National Security Council. The President's chief assistant, Marv Watson, made several trips to the publishers as they waited more than an hour, to assure them that the President was very interested in his meeting with them.[28]

President Johnson finally showed up, looking tired and dispirited. He had been struggling with issues of an unpopular war in a critical election year. Surprisingly, the President, in a relaxed manner, spent more than an hour having an open and honest conversation with what turned out to be one of his last meetings with a group of Negro leaders. He talked about how the senators from the South, Russell, Talmadge, Stennis, Fulbright, among others,

---

[27] According to Lawrence Allen Eldridge's *Chronicles of a Two-front War: Civil Rights and Vietnam in the African American Press*, President Johnson's daily diary, the NNPA met with President Johnson on March 15, 1968.

[28] W. Marvin "Marv" Watson was appointed postmaster general after serving as Johnson's Chief of Staff.

had accused him of being "a traitor" to the South based on his aggressive support of civil rights. He talked about how Negro leaders should have influence in both political parties.

He added how liberal Democratic senators from the North had urged him not to push a fair housing bill because, in their words, he has done enough in the area of civil rights and pushing a fair housing bill in the 1968 election year would be unpopular among some voters in northern states, important for a Democratic victory.

President Johnson told the publishers that he was undecided about the fair housing bill until one Sunday afternoon after church, he and Lady Bird, his wife, decided to take a trip on Air Force One to Georgia to see the 82nd Airborne soldiers off to Vietnam. Upon landing, as he was observing the troops, he noticed so many Negro soldiers. He said he walked up to one of them and asked, "Young man, what are your feelings about being in this group and going to Vietnam again?"

The soldier, standing erect, and with a strong voice, said, "Mr. President, I am from the South, and for the first time I have been treated as a first-class citizen, with respect and dignity." President Johnson said he was visibly impressed by the Negro soldier's comments.

The President said he and Lady Bird returned to the White House later that Sunday, said their prayers before going to bed. He said he got up the next morning and told Lady Bird that if those Negro soldiers could go to Vietnam and fight from an integrated bunker that he would do everything in his power, as their president, to make sure that when they returned home they could live in an integrated neighborhood. And that was his compelling rationale for his decision to push very hard for the passage of the Fair Housing Act of 1968.

From their perspective, some white historians, who were not at the White House meeting, will continue to write that it was entirely because of Vietnam that President Johnson decided not to run for re-election. President Johnson told the Negro publishers, his deep feeling was that he could not have carried the southern states in victory in 1968 as he did in the 1964 Presidential election against Republican candidate Barry Goldwater, because of his civil rights record.

X.

President Johnson from a Historical Perspective

I attended the 25th anniversary of the Great Society at the LBJ Library and Ranch in 1999.[29] At the closing dinner at the LBJ Ranch, hosted by his wife and two daughters, a video was played showing Mr. Johnson making his last public appearance at a seminar at the LBJ Library before his death. In his brief remarks, President Johnson said, almost in tears, that he was sorry that he could not have done more for American Negroes. This I think was a genuine testimony of President Lyndon Baines Johnson and his commitment to civil rights and the cause of Negro Americans.

At the three-day symposium on "The Legacy of the Sixties," sponsored by the Lyndon Baines Johnson Library and Museum, the LBJ School of Public Affairs and the University of Texas, several hundred members of the Johnson-Humphrey family of public servants who worked with him and

---

[29] Lyndon Baines Johnson.

journalists who covered him were invited to the symposium and reunion.[30] My invitation resulted from having served on the staff of Vice President Humphrey.

From the opening night's panel on "LBJ Remembered" to the concluding barbecue at the LBJ Ranch, the main focus was on the multifaceted personality, folksy humor, political persuasion, and restless determination of a president obsessed with doing as much as he could for Negroes, other minorities, the poor, the young, the aged, women, students, and workers in a short period of time.[31]

Noted historians Arthur Schlesinger, Jr., Doris Kearns Goodwin, and Michael Beschloss described President Johnson as the firmest ally of Blacks in the White House, as a revolutionary who used this great power to advance the cause of civil rights.

NAACP Chairman Julian Bond, and NAACP Legal Defense and Education Fund President Elaine R. Jones, who served on a civil rights panel, referred to President Johnson's push for the passage of the 1964 Civil Rights Act and the Voting Rights Act of

---

[30] The symposium was held May 12–14, 1999.

[31] The first panel on May 12, 1999 was shown on C-SPAN and was retrieved via https://www.c-span.org/video/?125507-1/lyndon-baines-johnson-remembered

1965 as "a defining moment of the civil rights movement in the 1960s."

Atty. Jones recalled, "I will never forget my commencement at Howard University, because President Johnson was the speaker who profoundly defined his civil rights goals in that historic speech on June 4, 1965." In that Howard University speech, President Johnson said:

> Freedom is not enough. You do not wipe away the scars of centuries by saying: Now you are free to go where you want, do as you desire, and choose the leaders you please.
>
> You do not take a person who, for years, has been hobbled by chains and liberate him, bring him up to the starting line of a race and then say, 'you are free to compete with all the others.' And still justly believe that you have been completely fair.
>
> Thus, it is not enough just to open the gates of opportunity. All our citizens must have the ability to walk through those gates. This is the next and more profound stage of the battle for civil rights. We seek not just freedom but opportunity—not just legal equity but human ability, not just equality as a right and a theory, but equality as a fact and as a result.[32]

---

[32] Lyndon B. Johnson, "Commencement Address at Howard University Lyndon B. Johnson," *The U.S. Constitution: A Reader* (Michigan: Hillsdale College Press, 2012), pp. 765–772. President Johnson's complete commencement address is available at https://online.hillsdale.edu/document.doc?id=286

As panelists, former members of the LBJ White House, Bill Moyers, Jack Valenti, Joseph A. Califano, Jr., Jim Jones and George Christian had many funny stories to tell about "a man who was compassionate and cold and calculating, brave and brazen, urbanely polite and uncannily profane." They all agreed that LBJ harnessed the social energy of that time and used his great legislative skills and persuasive powers to pass legislation that helped those from the cradle to the grave.

In my humble judgment, President Abraham Lincoln does not come anywhere near President Johnson's record of having Black Americans voting, working, eating, shopping, riding, attending school, and spending where and as they were never able to do before.

Unfortunately, in 2008, in the centennial celebration of President Johnson's birth, at the Democratic National Convention in Denver, Colorado, there was not a single reference to President Johnson and his historic contributions to improving American's democracy for its minority citizens and job liberation of women. This, I thought, was shameful of the Democratic Party and its leadership.

There was only a small turnout of about 300 friends and former staff and supporters at the centennial celebration of his birth at the Mayflower

Hotel in Washington, D.C. In a few years after his death, President Johnson's historic record on civil rights was forgotten by so many who benefitted.

An Elderly Mississippi Man and His Profile of Courage

If my recollection is accurate, I think it was Vernon Jordan, as director of the Voter Education Project, who described an elderly Black man voting for the first time in the hostile environment of Mississippi.[33]

The man, a 70-plus-year-old sharecropper in Greenville, Mississippi, joined dozens of Blacks standing in a long line to register to vote. He was wearing neatly pressed coveralls and leaned on a self-made cane. The old man ignored the angry shouts of the white crowd and the sneers from rednecks in sheriff uniforms.

On this hot summer day, these Negroes, about 100 of them, had come to the county clerk's office to register to vote, many of them for the first time.

The old man, bent over like an old oak tree, every so often pulled out a large red handkerchief to mop the sweat from his brow. As the old man stood

---

[33] Vernon Jordan served as the second executive director of the Voter Education Project.

there, waiting to register to vote, a white reporter for a northern newspaper, approached him. The reporter asked, in a friendly voice, "Mister, pardon me, but may I ask you a couple of questions?"

The old man looked up at the reporter, paused, and quietly nodded his approval. The reporter asked, "Mister, have you ever registered to vote before in your life?"

Without looking at the reporter, the old man shook his head and said, "No sur." The reporter paused and then asked, "Mister, why, why do you risk your life at your age to register to vote for the first time?"

The old man lifted his head and looked at the reporter, with tired eyes that glowed in the bright sunshine.

"Sur," the old man began, "I wuz always told by my daddy to beware of trouble acoming, of trouble acoming."

The old man paused, wiped away the dripping sweat from his face, and said, with his head tilted in the sun, "Sur, but trouble acoming ain't acoming like it usta did...trouble acoming ain't acoming like it usta did."

For me, this old man had the strength, the fortitude, the intense commitment to face up to the tremendous odds and obstacles of his time like so many brave Negroes in Mississippi during the height of the civil right movement and violence.

Without the civil rights efforts of President Johnson, I don't think Dr. King would have emerged as a civil rights hero. Because of President Johnson's signing of the Voting Rights bill, this brought a new era of political empowerment to Negroes in the South. Also, the results of the Voting Rights bill might have been part of the foundation for the election of our first Black President. All of this is or could be a part of the great legacy, yet to be understood and appreciated by the public, of President Lyndon Baines Johnson.

XI.

Surprising Appointment to the Staff of Vice President Hubert H. Humphrey

A tremendous shock was my appointment to Vice President Hubert H. Humphrey's staff. This was something quietly orchestrated by Hobart Taylor, Jr. and Louis Martin. This resulted from an item in the *Jet* magazine column of Simeon Booker about the two white liberals of Washington, Vice President Humphrey and New York Senator Robert Kennedy, not having a single Negro on their staffs.

Senator Kennedy wasted no time in appointing Earl Graves to manage his Harlem, New York office.

I have no evidence of this, but Vice President Humphrey's office began a national search for a highly qualified Negro for his staff, interviewing a judge and attorneys. The search ended when the Vice President had a telephone conversation with Hobart Taylor, Jr., whose judgment was well respected. Hobart mentioned to Mr. Humphrey a journalist from Detroit who could be helpful to him if he ever decided to run for president. Hobart advised him to call Louis Martin, since the journalist worked for Martin's newspaper, the *Michigan Chronicle*, in Detroit. Mr. Humphrey did have that conversation with Martin, who reinforced Taylor's recommendation. That is all Vice President Humphrey needed.

Without even meeting and interviewing the journalist from Detroit, the Vice President advised his staff to meet with the journalist and began the process of vetting, FBI security clearance, and adding him to the staff.

The next thing I knew is one of my female friends in Detroit was called by the FBI to check on my character. I said to her, "My dear, I hope you were somewhat positive in your response." We both laughed. And, sure enough, I was cleared by the FBI and later appointed to the staff of Vice President Humphrey...

I did not meet the Vice President until weeks later at a VIP reception for business executives at the Department of State. His assistant, John G. Stewart, and Press Secretary Norman Sherman, introduced me to the Vice President. He shook my hand and called the media over and said, "This is Ofield Dukes and he is a new member of my staff." And that was the photo mailed with the news release that dozens of Black newspapers carried.

In a subsequent private meeting with Vice President Humphrey in his office at the U.S. Capitol, he sat behind his desk, under a huge chandelier, signing letters. I took notes of his words: "Ofield, I am pleased to have you on my staff. Public service is an honor. Life has been good to me, but there is so much to be done, a lot of work to do. I want you to use good judgment, take the initiative, do it in my name, but whatever you do, don't make me look bad."

One of my first assignments was assisting in writing a speech for him for the annual national conference of the NAACP in Los Angeles. What I added at the end of his speech were excerpts from the National Negro Anthem. The Vice President was especially thrilled over the thousands of NAACP delegates giving him a standing ovation...but I did not indicate that the delegates stood up in honor of their national anthem.

On his staff, I served as associate press secretary, and handled youth, civil rights, and all kinds of other issues. He would sometimes call early in the morning with various assignments.

Hubert H. Humphrey, The Man

Friday, May 27, 2011, marked the 100th anniversary of the birth of Hubert H. Humphrey.

But according to a column by Rick Perlstein, headlined, "America's Forgotten Liberal," he wrote, "no one besides me seems to have noticed."[34]

This is a dark mark, a tragic missing page in contemporary American history.

HHH was a vibrant, caring, humanistic, super liberal, devoted to civil rights and intensely devoted to public service. As mayor of Minneapolis, he was one of the first mayors in the country to champion fair employment practices legislation. He gained national attention and popularity at the National Democratic Convention, in 1948, in Philadelphia, when he bolted the platform of the party by leading the fight for a minor platform strongly supporting civil rights. His courageous efforts led to Senator Strom Thurman, of South Carolina, walking out of the convention and organizing a southern white wing of the Democratic Party.

For Humphrey, civil rights, treating your neighbor as you would treat God, was more than a political belief. This was his credo, a way of life taught to him by his father. It became part of his

---

[34] Rick Perstein's *New York Times* opinion editorial on May 27, 2011 compared the 100th anniversary of Humphrey's birth to the major fanfare associated with Ronald Reagan's 100th birth anniversary in January 2011. Rick Perstein, "America's Forgotten Liberal," *New York Times,* May 27, 2011, A27. Retrieved from http://www.nytimes.com/2011/05/27/opinion/27Perlstein.html

practicing religion. He was a man of sheer courage, full of enthusiasm for a battle on civil and human rights.

He was a person of restless energy, an insatiable desire to do more as a public servant. When he lived in Southwest Washington, he would ride to work and see dirty streets, stop his car and called D.C. officials to complain and insist on immediate action to correct the problem.

On one occasion, I arranged for Humphrey to meet Marion Barry, co-founder of a social service group called Pride with a contract to kill rodents in the District. Humphrey met Barry and his workers in a filthy, back alley in Washington's ghetto to find out what he could do to help such a situation. Humphrey became angry over what he observed. Humphrey became so interested in the District of Columbia that he arranged for playfields to have lights and invited the Supremes to assist him in dedicating portable swimming pools in the poorest wards.[35] Humphrey informally became known as the District of Columbia's "Mayor-at-Large."

Humphrey, of course, was quite a speaker, an orator. I recall his speaking to a group of more than

---

[35] The Supremes endorsed Hubert H. Humphrey for President after the death of Robert Kennedy, according to *The Supremes: A Saga of Motown Dreams, Success, and Betrayal* by Mark Ribowsky.

500 ministers during the 1968 presidential campaign at Cobo Hall in Detroit.[36] This was HHH at his oratorical best in inspiring the ministers to standing and shouting amen.[37] At the end of his remarks, I think it was A.M.E. Bishop H.H. Brookins who stood on a chair and began singing the "Battle Hymn of the Republic."[38] And Humphrey stood at the podium and wept.

Sometimes Humphrey, in his enthusiasm, misspoke. In a speech before the Jaycees in Detroit, he talked about a "Marshall Plan" and was publicly reprimanded by President Johnson. In a New Orleans speech, the Vice President said he has enough spunk to lead a riot, which generated a negative public reaction.

In spite of his differences with President Johnson, Humphrey complimented Johnson's commitment to civil rights and led the bitter battle for the passage of Title VII. As previously referenced, Humphrey spent days and nights at his office at the U.S. Capitol badgering reluctant

---

[36] The notes of Democratic rally on October 6, 1966 in Detroit is retrieved from http://www2.mnhs.org/library/findaids/00442/pdfa/00442-02016.pdf.

[37] Hubert H. Humphrey was at times referred to as HHH in documents that staff wrote.

[38] The African Methodist Episcopal (A.M.E.)

senators to support the civil rights bill. And, unfortunately, he has not received his due for his exceptional work and political leadership.

Hubert H. Humphrey was a great American of the highest order, a dedicated public servant who dedicated his life to improving the quality of life for those in greatest need. Of course, he was more qualified to be president than Richard Milhous Nixon. Working as part of his professional staff was a remarkable experience.

Unfortunately, Humphrey's staff and supporters were unhappy about how they felt President Johnson treated the Vice President.

Experiences on the Staff of Vice President Humphrey

Serving on the Vice President's staff was a thrilling, a tremendous learning and politically enriching experience. I traveled with him on a nine-country trip to Africa in 1967, on another trip to Korea for the inauguration of that country's president and throughout America. During the 1968 presidential campaign, I was a member of the traveling staff.

While on his staff, Soul Brother Number One, James Brown called, complaining that Bob Hope was always invited to entertain American troops. He wanted to do the same. So, I called the USO official at the Pentagon. The official had never heard of James Brown. I mentioned it to the Vice President, who became incensed and made a call. The official called back. I arranged for James Brown to entertain the troops in Vietnam. *Jet* magazine featured an article on the break through.

Introduction of Dr. Leon Sullivan to Vice President Humphrey and President Johnson

On another occasion, I received a call about having Dr. Leon Sullivan, founder of the Opportunity Industrialization Centers (OIC) job training program and leader out of Philadelphia of a bread boycott, to meet the Vice President. So, I called Vi Williams (Biglane), Humphrey's scheduling secretary, who said he was very busy but have Dr. Sullivan to meet me in his outer office for Humphrey to say a quick hello to him.

Sullivan, a towering man with a booming baritone voice, met me at the Humphrey Office. When the Vice President returned from a National Security meeting at the White House, he rushed into his office. Dr. Sullivan and I were taken into the Vice President's office as he, the Vice President, spoke to his wife on the phone. When he hung up, he jumped up and I introduced him to Dr. Sullivan as he headed toward the door, rushing to another meeting.

Dr. Sullivan began talking, "Mr. Vice President, it's not the altitude of a person that counts, but his or her attitude..." Humphrey stopped to listen. In a matter of two or three minutes, Humphrey was wiping a tear from his eyes. He asked, "What manner of man is this?" He then dashed to his desk, called Hobart Taylor, Jr. and said he wanted Dr. Sullivan to speak on his behalf at a Plans for Progress meeting of America's top corporate executives the next day. He was so impressed with Dr. Sullivan.

At the Plans for Progress meeting, Dr. Sullivan had the corporate executives on their feet with his brilliant speech about his job training programs in cities throughout the country.

Early the next morning, the Vice President called me at home and asked me to develop a memo for President Johnson on Dr. Sullivan and his OIC program. I rushed to the office, did the memo and sent it to the Vice President. He, in turn, sent it to President Johnson. Two weeks later, President Johnson took Air Force One to Philadelphia to meet with Dr. Sullivan in Dr. Sullivan's office in an old jail house. From that moment on, Dr. Sullivan's OIC budget was a line item in the annual budget of a U.S. President.

This resulted in a close working relationship with Dr. Sullivan. I became his close friend, advisor and consultant, especially during his fight to end apartheid in South Africa. (I recall efforts of lobbyists for South Africa using funds to try to project a most positive image for that country and my refusal to be part of that devious campaign.)

Advisor to Dr. Leon Sullivan and his Fight to End Apartheid in South Africa

Dr. Sullivan was the founder of the Opportunities Industrialization Centers and organized chapters throughout the country to promote job training. He was a towering man from West Virginia, with a strong voice, tremendous confidence in his ability to make a difference in the lives of Negro Americans.

In addition, he became one of the most aggressive advocates of Africa, in sponsoring summit meetings in various countries. I attended one of his summit meetings in Gabon, Africa. And the attendance was so great that there was no hotel space for me, and even Ossie Davis and his wife, Ruby Dee. And we all had to sleep on the floor that night until the hotel found rooms for us.

Dr. Sullivan's main focus became South Africa and his development of Sullivan Principles as guidelines for American firms doing business in a country where Black people were oppressed under a mean form of slavery, apartheid.

I served as Dr. Sullivan's public relations advisor and handled all his media and public relations activities whenever he came to Washington.

I remember on one occasion he called and asked, "Brother Dukes, what are people saying about our work?" I told him frankly, "Dr. Sullivan, some people are saying you need to come home, instead of spending so much time in Africa, because the problems in the American ghetto are just as acute."

At an OIC convention in Minnesota, I was pleased to receive a special award from Dr. Sullivan and OIC in Minneapolis, January 1988, which read in part, "For Service to His Fellow Man and Through Excellence in the Field of Public Relations."

Our friendship was so close that on the day Dr. Sullivan died, his wife called from Scottsdale, Arizona. She said her late husband requested me to assist in coordinating his funeral arrangements.[39] And that I did.

Vice President Humphrey's spirit of voluntary public service was contagious and he encouraged his staff to take advantage of any opportunity to render a public service. And this was something I looked forward to doing. Some of the projects included the

---

[39] *Jet* magazine on May 21, 2001 chronicled Ofield Dukes' responsibility to arrange the funeral. "National Headliners," *Jet*, May 21, 2011, p. 10.

Washington Urban League's School Drop-Out Campaign.

District of Columbia Public Relations and Civic Involvement

Vice President Humphrey's spirit of voluntary public service was contagious and he encouraged his staff to take advantage of any opportunity to render a public service. And this was something I looked forward to doing.

In 1967, the Washington Urban League launched a campaign to reduce the incidence of high school drop-outs in the D.C. public school system.[40] As a member of the staff of Vice President Hubert H. Humphrey, I became involved.

At the time, James Brown, Soul Brother #1, was calling about going to Vietnam, like Bob Hope, to entertain our troops. I mentioned to him about the Urban League's anti-school drop-out campaign. Mr. Brown offered to come to Washington to support the campaign if I would do one thing for him—have a photo taken with the Vice President. That I promised.

---

[40] Lyndon Johnson Proclamation 3801—"Stay in School"—describes the campaign
http://www.presidency.ucsb.edu/ws/index.php?pid=106041

Mr. Brown came and with a new song, "Don't Be a Drop-Out," that hit the Billboard charts and became a hit.[41] And he was a big hit in Washington in urging students not to drop-out of school. The campaign for the Washington Urban League was so successful that the school system had problems finding teachers to handle students returning to school.

I did arrange for Mr. Brown to have a photo taken with Vice President Humphrey and the ingenious businessman used the photos on billboards to promote his concerts. I really liked Mr. Brown. He was such a polite and humble gentleman, always referring to me as Mr. Dukes.

Exciting Trip to Africa

In 1967, I had the wonderful opportunity of joining Vice President Humphrey on a VIP tour of nine African countries, with the first being the inauguration of the Republic of Liberia's President, William Tubman. This included a visit with the celebrated Man of Juda, Ethiopian Emperor Haile Salassie. This was my first visit to the native land.

In Monrovia, Liberia, on the night of President Tubman's inaugural dinner, then Solicitor General

---

[41] "Don't Be a Drop-Out" recorded by James Brown was his first attempt at a socially conscious song, encouraging teenagers to stay in school. https://en.wikipedia.org/wiki/Don't_Be_a_Drop-Out

Thurgood Marshall came back to the hotel in a rage. We were all gathered in my hotel room, on New Year's Eve, and I was being ribbed for having some Hershey candy bars on my desk and accused of bringing the candy bars to Africa to curry female favors. Of course, this was not true. Mr. Marshall was angry because the inaugural dinner was so disorganized, due to the Liberian Chief of Protocol allegedly being drunk. On this hot, humid night, Mr. Marshall was attired in formal attire and there was no air conditioning at the dinner. He was most creative in his use of curse words.

During our African trip, we made a gas stop in the Shalles Island where I met a beautiful, tan-complexioned, green-eyed young lady. In our conversation, I asked if she wanted to visit the United States. Her response was emphatic.

"Absolutely no!" she said. "Why should I? I don't need to see the slums of New York or Los Angeles. My county is more beautiful."

Her message was very clear and I understood it.

Representing Vice President Humphrey in a 1967 Trip to Jackson, Mississippi

Dr. Aaron Henry, as president of the Mississippi NAACP, had invited Vice President Humphrey to Jackson, Mississippi to address the meeting of the NAACP and the Mississippi Freedom Now (Democratic) Party. Humphrey had a scheduling conflict and he decided to send me to represent him.

Dr. Henry presided over the morning session of the NAACP, where I had brief remarks on behalf of the Vice President. It was an extraordinary experience for me to meet and speak with Medgar Evers, Director of the Mississippi NAACP and Fannie Lou Hamer.

At noon, Dr. Evers adjourned the meeting of the NAACP and promptly convened a meeting of the Mississippi Freedom Now Party, organized by Black Democrats in Mississippi because Blacks were shut out of the main Democratic Party by white politicians.

I left Mississippi with tremendous respect for the political ingenuity and courage of Dr. Henry, Medgar Evers, Fannie Lou Hamer and other civil rights and political activists in Mississippi. Today, there are more Black-elected officials in Mississippi than any other state in America. This is the legacy of Dr. Henry, who was a pharmacist, Medgar Evers, Fannie Lou Hamer and those who gave their lives for the civil rights of Blacks in that state and in our country.

1968 Presidential Campaign

And there was the 1968 presidential campaign of which I was actively involved. So many unforgettable experiences.

Louis Martin, as vice chairman of the Democratic National Committee, had a fellow named Dr. Ronald Walters call me about becoming involved in the 1968 presidential campaign.[42] I responded by getting him involved in the District of Columbia campaign. I suspect that was the beginning of the brilliant political career of Dr. Ronald Walters.

At the Howard University one-day symposium (April 5, 2011) on the 40th anniversary of the Congressional Black Caucus, Dr. Walters was honored for his strategic work with the Congressional Black Caucus and his national political leadership and contributions. He chaired Rev. Jesse Jackson's presidential campaign in 1988 and was chairman of the Political Science Department at Howard University and the author of several books.

There was the assignment of getting James Brown to endorse Humphrey. I had several telephone calls with James Brown who was anxious

---

[42] Pronounced Louie. Ofield would often write his nickname Louie in the original version. However, for consistency and clarity, Louis is used as others pronounced Louis, Louie, in general.

to buy a radio station in Georgia. By chance, Brown
and Humphrey would be in Los Angeles at the same
time. So, I arranged for James Brown to come to
Humphrey's rally in Watts and for he and Humphrey
to dance on stage together, the Boogaloo.

Subsequently, I went to Philadelphia to follow
up to get Brown to publicly endorse Humphrey, but
he was not available. Later, through the efforts of
Robert Brown, a Black supporter of GOP candidate
Richard Milhous Nixon, Brown promised Nixon
support for assisting Brown in purchasing several
radio stations in Georgia. That deal appealed to
Brown, who announced his support of Nixon, to my
chagrin and that of Humphrey.

In another incident, while campaigning in
Newark, New Jersey, two Black activists, a
prominent poet from New Jersey and college
professor from Los Angeles, approached me and said
Humphrey would not be allowed to campaign
peacefully in South Los Angeles, Watts, without any
disruptions from the Blackstone Rangers, if
somehow funds were not contributed to support the
election of the first Black mayor of Newark,
Kenneth Gibson.[43] So, I secretly made a call for

---

[43] The Blackstone Rangers of Chicago had a reputation of being
both a street gang and "a constructive engine of community Black
power." "Chicago's Blackstone Rangers (I)," *The Atlantic*, May
1969, retrieved from

funds to be delivered in the middle of the night to a special contact in Denver as a contribution to Gibson's campaign. And Humphrey did have a peaceful campaign visit in Los Angeles, at which Humphrey met and danced with James Brown.[44]

I recall the last weekend of the campaign in Los Angeles. I had called singer Nancy Wilson about contacting Congress members Andy Young and John Conyers who were reluctant about supporting Humphrey because of his position supporting the Vietnam War. Nancy suggested meeting her after her last performance at a famous night club where she was appearing, after 2 a.m.

---

https://www.theatlantic.com/magazine/archive/1969/05/chicagos-blackstone-rangers-i/305741/. However, the off-shoot of the Blackstone Rangers in which Rev. John Fry had been associated in Chicago before relocating to California became known the Black P. Stones, Black P. Stone Nation, BPSN or Blackstones in the 1960s in California according to George W. Knox, "Gang Profile Update: The Black P. Stone Nation (BPSN)," http://www.ngcrc.com/bpsn2003.html.

[44] "James Brown Interviews about Hubert Humphrey and the Black Panthers," video on dailymotion.com, 1:13, from the documentary "The Night James Brown Saved Boston," posted by "anyclip," April 4, 2013, http://www.dailymotion.com/video/xyu7wz_james-brown-interviews-about-hubert-humphrey-and-the-black-panthers-from-james-brown-black-panthers_shortfilms. The video shows James Brown and Vice President Humphrey together.

Pseudo White Liberals

So, I went there, and Nancy placed calls to Young and Conyers and held long conversations with them. In her dressing room were several movie executives. When Nancy introduced me as a member of Humphrey's staff, these white executives expressed their own concerns about Humphrey and his busing of school children, of his pushing fair employment, and open housing. It then occurred to me that Humphrey was too liberal even for so-called white liberals. And this was dramatically and tragically confirmed when the most liberal white organizations, Americans for Democratic Action (ADA), refused, along with liberal Senator Eugene McCarthy, to endorse him because of his support for President Johnson's Vietnam War policies.

The tragic paradox is that Humphrey co-founded the ADA. I was baffled over how could his closest friends and political allies turn their backs on him and rather allow Richard Milhous Nixon become president. What type of liberalism is this? What type of political hierocracy is this? Unbelievable!

As President Johnson feared about his candidacy in 1968 because of his position on civil rights, Humphrey did not carry a single southern state in the election.

Personal Reflections On 1968 Presidential Campaign

On Saturday, November 9, 1968, I wrote
personal observations about my experiences as a
member of the campaign staff of Democratic
presidential candidate, Hubert H. Humphrey:

> After more than eight months of physical,
> emotional, and spiritual involvement in the Vice
> President's campaign for the presidency, I feel a
> great sense of relief, a feeling of being emancipated
> from the demands and pressures, mental and
> physical, of the campaign.
>
> In looking back, in reflection on the thousands of
> miles we traveled, and the thousands of man-hours
> and millions of dollars spent, I wonder if there is a
> more sane and practical way to elect a president of
> the United States. Not to mention the tragedy of
> last June, the death of Senator Robert Kennedy in
> the presidential primary in California.
>
> With this feeling of relief is a feeling of remorse,
> or sadness, of disappointment over one thing in
> particular: the way Hubert Humphrey was treated by
> his friends, the professional politicians, the so-called
> liberal wing of the Democratic Party, college
> students angry over the unpopular war in Vietnam,
> and what I consider the unfair judgment of
> American voters. I say unfair because the issues of
> ability, competence, integrity, demonstrated
> leadership, commitment to public service were
> clouded by Humphrey's support for President

Johnson and the Vietnam War. Then there were those in the North who felt that Humphrey was too liberal on school busing and fair housing.

This was a terrible paradox for Humphrey for not supporting a president who became as intensely committed to the cause of civil rights for American Negroes as he was.

Even in defeat, Humphrey was magnificent. It was remarkable that he was able to bear so many crosses and struggled from so far behind to almost win.

The political game of politics at the presidential level can be so vindictive and vicious. Those who have been offended by members of their own party may rather suffer bitter and inglorious defeat than yield on a meaningless issue or point of principle. Alliances and allegiances are rigidly defined and kept. Political territorial boundaries are sacred and must be protected.

Media reporters are another interesting fraternity. Some are highly professional and dedicated to covering the news objectively. Others are prima donnas, always complaining. A few have biased views, are self-styled experts, false guardians of the truth and are patently unfair in their coverage.

In attending the chaotic, violent Democratic national convention in Chicago, it was such a political tragedy for Humphrey, the Democratic presidential candidate, to bear the cross of tens of thousands of predominantly white college students demonstrating against the Vietnam War and the convention. The bloody battle between the students and Mayor Richard Daley's brutal law enforcement was a daily news feature on national television. Such ugly images! But Humphrey, the happy, determined warrior, made a gallant fight to the bitter end and almost won the election, coming from behind in the polls. He said if he had a couple more days, he would have won.

The last-minute chicanery of the leadership of South Vietnam not to negotiate a settlement of the war before the election did not help Humphrey at all.

Democratic Party Taking the Black Vote for Granted

I was struck by the irony of the Black vote being solid and strong for Humphrey, in spite of the fact that there was very limited involvement of Blacks in the inner-circle of Humphrey's campaign. The campaign used as high visibility surrogates Jackie Robinson, Rafer Johnson, Chubby Checker, civil rights leader Charles Evers, Patricia Harris, and some elected officials.[45] But none had a special relationship with the candidate. Louis Martin, as deputy director of the Democratic National Committee, was the one

---

[45] Rafer Johnson was a decathlon athlete and actor.

Black who provided strategic advice to the Humphrey campaign.

An unfortunate fact of Democratic politics is how the Black vote is taken for granted. That was the case in 1968 and I think that still remains the case in 2011. The adage is Black voters produce the ballots and whites produce the bucks. And those sitting around the table making decisions are those who produce the bucks.

It wasn't until Charles T. Manatt became chairman of the Democratic National Committee that the question was raised about no Blacks or a conspicuous few serving on the influential Democratic Finance Committee. A minimum of $15,000 is required to join the committee.

I was flying to Los Angeles for a business meeting when, by chance, I met Manatt on the plane. We started talking and he said he was interested in having Blacks recruited to serve on the Finance Committee. I indicated that I would discuss that with Louis Martin, as deputy chair of the Democratic Committee.

When we arrived at the Los Angeles airport, Manatt asked about my destination and then was kind enough to have his chauffeur to drive me to my destination in Bel Air. He was a kind, gentleman, a very wealthy man with a large law firm in Los Angeles.

When I returned to Washington, I did have that conversation with Martin, and we began recruiting Blacks for the Finance Committee. My first call was to Don King, who sent his check to Manatt. And this was a great investment for my client, who subsequently was invited to dinner at the White House by President Jimmy Carter, one of the perks of being a member of the DNC Finance Committee. According to my records, I recruited a number of Blacks to join the DNC Finance Committee, totaling more than 100.

What a great lesson this has been for me in American presidential politics.

I deeply regret reading in *The Washington Post* today, Sunday, July 23, 2011, the death of Manatt on July 22 at the age of 75, after suffering a stroke. *The Post's* article describes how Manatt, as chairman of the Democratic National Committee, overcame the party $2 million debt, raised $6 million to build a permanent Capitol Hill Democratic headquarters and strengthened the political structure of the party.

After the Humphrey election campaign, I spent several agonizing months pondering my future. I went to New York for an interview with IBM, which did not appeal to me. There was a young lady in Detroit waiting for my return to marry her. But I had no job and was not prepared to assume that kind of responsibility. What was my fate? What could I do in Washington?

XII.

Entry into the Field of Public Relations

It was a perfect spring day in April of 1969. I stepped out on my balcony of my apartment in Southwest Washington and was inspired by the cherry blossoms in full bloom, by the beautiful blue skies, and the chirping of birds. While standing there, I had an epiphany, a sudden realization of a career path. The thought erupted in my mind: why not remain in Washington and set up a little public relations tent. Within two weeks, I had withdrawn my federal retirement funds of $2,500, subleased space at the National Press Building with a part-time secretary, and opened Ofield Dukes & Associates. I always wanted to be my own boss.

Shortly after the opening of my PR firm, Mrs. Esther Gordy Edwards[46] called. The sister of

---

[46] Sister to Motown Founder, Esther Gordy Edwards is the founder of Motown Museum and a former Motown Records' senior vice president and corporate secretary.
https://www.motownmuseum.org/about-the-museum/the-museum/esther-gordy-edwards/

Motown's Berry Gordy[47] said, "Hey, Ofield, Motown would like to be your first client..." My response was, "How wonderful!" My second client was soap manufacturer Lever Brothers, because of a previous contact I had with the company's vice president for public relations.

The recession of 1971 had its impact. I was on my own payroll at $50 per week. This was a very difficult time of survival. There were days when I did not have 50 cents to catch the bus from my apartment in Southwest Washington to the Press Building. So, I walked. There were weekends when my kitchen cupboard was bare. I had a female friend who was good at cooking chili and kept me from starving. The mental and physical pressure was so great that I was hospitalized as a result of hypertension and stress. During a one-week stay at Georgetown Hospital, a prominent cardiologist advised me to take steps to overcome this hypertension. So, I took a course in Transcendental Meditation and began playing tennis.

Business during those early years was dismal. White PR professionals and possible white potential clients still saw me as an upstart majoring in Black public relations. Although I became accredited in my

---

[47] Berry Gordy Jr. founded Motown Records in 1959.
https://www.motownmuseum.org/story/berry-gordy/

fifth year and won the "Oscar" in public relations in my seventh year, the perception was still there.[48] It stung when some potential Black clients met with me, asked for my PR recommendations, and then literally shut the door in my face. Opening my PR office in the National Press Building brought me within walking distance to the White House and the Johnson Publishing Company. I joined the Public Relations Society of America in 1973 and took the examination for accreditation and passed it, but I was still perceived as a limited specialist in "Black public relations." At the time, there were no other Black PR practitioners in D.C. with a downtown office. There were individual Blacks in public relations, but they were virtually invisible.

A major source of encouragement and support came from Al Fleishman,[49] a founder of one of the largest PR firms in the country, Fleishman-Hillard.

---

[48] Accredited in Public Relations is a professional designation earned through the Public Relations Society of America in conjunction now with the Universal Accreditation Board. Silver Anvil Award from the Public Relations Society of America is often considered the "Oscar" of the public relations industry recognizing the top public relations campaigns in multiple industry sectors. Ofield Dukes won the Silver Anvil for his 1973 campaign inaugurating Detroit's First African-American mayor.

[49] Alfred "Al" Fleishman was co-founder, with business partner Robert Hillard, of Fleishman-Hillard.

Mr. Fleishman called to offer advice and sent me excellent publications that he had authored on public and community relations. Anheuser-Busch was a major client of Fleishman-Hillard and eventually Anheuser-Bush became one of my clients. As important and busy as he was, Mr. Fleishman was generous of his time and genuine in his friendship with me. He has since passed, but I will always remember the positive impact he had on my fledging public relations life in the early 1970s.

Public Relations Project Challenges

I discovered there is no substitute for actual experience. And it was that actual experience that advanced substantially my learning curve and professional development.

Founding of Congressional Black Caucus—First CBC Dinner

In 1971, Rep. Charles C. Diggs, Jr., as the senior Black member of the U.S. Congress, called about having me and my firm handles the public relations for the founding of the Congressional Black Caucus and the first fundraising dinner scheduled for June

18. Al Nellum,[50] President of A.L. Nellum &
Associates, assumed great leadership in planning and
managing the first dinner of the Congressional Black
Caucus.

Having a close friendship with Rep. Diggs, since
we both were from Detroit, I was aware of his
concern that President Richard Milhous Nixon, who
refused to meet with Black members of Congress,
might dismantle the historic civil rights legislation
and Great Society programs under the leadership of
President Johnson.

Ms. Carolyn P. DuBose, a former press secretary
to Rep. Diggs, describes, in her well-researched book
on Mr. Diggs, how he began and went through a
deliberate process in organizing the Congressional
Black Caucus.

In her book, *The Untold Story of Charles Diggs*,[51]
Ms. DuBose quoted Mr. Diggs as saying, "I started
the Democratic Select committee in 1969. The next

---

[50] Albert L. Nellum, who founded A.L. Nellum and Associates in
1964 and operated the consulting firm until he retired in the early
1990s, died March 1 at the Heritage Hall health-care and
rehabilitation center in Leesburg, Va.
https://www.washingtonpost.com/local/obituaries/albert-l-nellum-
consulting-firm-founder/2014/03/11/13577a2a-a561-11e3-a5fa-
55f0c77bf39c_story.html?utm_term=.cae66c219578

[51] Carolyn DuBose, *The Untold Story of Charles Diggs*, (Arlington, Va.:
Barton Pub. House, 1998), p. 79.

step in the process that came out of that was the Congressional Black Caucus."

Added Mr. Diggs, "They did not call me. I am the one who called them. I am the guy that called the meetings. I deliberately did not come in there, Pharaoh-style. I wanted the thing to come up through the group to set the pattern about what they wanted to do. I set in my own mind a time limit. If they were just going to be meeting and having a few drinks or something, I certainly did not want it to develop into something like that."[52]

In addition to a climate of White House hostility, 1971 was a year of an economic recession. In the civil right movement, there emerged a militant Black Power movement led by Stokely Carmichael and H. Rap Brown, who advocated meeting the violence of Alabama Sheriff Bull Connor and Alabama Governor George Wallace with Black violence, contrary to the non-violence approach of Dr. Martin Luther King, Jr.[53]

---

[52] Carolyn DuBose, *The Untold Story of Charles Diggs*, (Arlington, Va: Barton Pub. House, 1998), pp. 79–80.

[53] Stokely Carmichael is also known as Kwame Ture. H. Rap Brown succeeded Stokely Carmichael as chairman of the Student Nonviolent Coordinating Committee (SNCC) and was a prominent figure in the Black Panther Party. A leading proponent of Black Power and a polarizing media icon, Brown symbolized both the power and the dangers—for white Americans and for radical activists themselves—of the civil rights movement's new

With the publicity surrounding the establishment of the Congressional Black Caucus, there was fear and anxiety in the white community, especially among business executives, in linking such a radical effort by Black members in the U.S. Congress with the Black Power movement.

I was in the second year of operating my public relations firm out of the National Press Building when Rep. Diggs made a special call out of concern for white and even Black perceptions associating the Congressional Black Caucus with the Black power movement.

Rep. Diggs and I discussed the strategy of my convening a press conference at the National Press Club that would involve CBC members Reps. Louis Stokes and Bill Clay.[54] At the well-attended press conference, Reps. Stokes and Clay eloquently clarified the political objectives of the Black Caucus and the first dinner.

---

militancy in the late 1960s. http://www.blackpast.org/aah/brown-hubert-h-rap-jamil-abdullah-al-amin-1943#sthash.Ur779lrm.dpuf. Theophilus Eugene Connor, known as Bull Connor, served as an elected Commissioner of Public Safety for Birmingham, Alabama, for more than 20 years, standing in strong opposition to the 1960s American Civil Rights Movement.

[54] Louis Stokes (D-Ohio) served 15 terms in the House of Representatives and was first Black congressional representative elected in Ohio. William Lacy "Bill" Clay, Sr. (D-Missouri) represented Missouri's First District which includes portions of St. Louis, for 32 years.

A syndicated white columnist had written that the CBC dinner in June could be raising funds in support of a CBC member planning to run for president. The suggested candidate was Rep. John Conyers, Jr., although Rep. Shirley Chisholm actually ran for president in 1972.[55]

In my initial news release on the CBC dinner, I wrote: "Funds from the $100 per plate banquet will be used by the Caucus to finance a permanent, independent staff to conduct in depth analysis of issues and policies relevant to Black and poor America."

The news release continued: "In a formal statement, the Caucus said, 'Rumors, news reports, editorials and other media statements are appearing frequently, implying sponsorship of the dinner is related to secret plans in support of a Black member of congress for the presidency in the 1972 elections. The Congressional Black Caucus categorically denies that any money raised by us at this affair will go to support one, Black or white, Democrat, Republican,

---

[55] Congressman Conyers (D-Michigan) was a founding member of the Congressional Black Caucus. https://conyers.house.gov/about/short-biography. Shirley Chisholm also was a founding member of the Congressional Black Caucus (CBC) in 1971 and the Congressional Women's Caucus in 1977. http://history.house.gov/People/Listing/C/CHISHOLM,-Shirley-Anita-(C000371)/

3rd party or 4th party who is a candidate for the presidency."

As far as the first CBC dinner and my firm handling the public relations, there was some concern about people paying as much as $100 to attend such a dinner. That was quite a sum of money at that time. But at the dinner,[56] there was an overwhelming crowd. The Sheraton-Park Hotel ballroom had a capacity of 2,400, with 24 tables for 10 persons. There were 2,800 who crowded into the ballroom, a standing room only crowd.

We did have an anxious moment at the hotel when the fire marshal threatened to do something about the safety of such an overflow crowd. With people outside the ballroom trying to get in, moving people out of the ballroom would have been a public relations disaster, possibly leading to a riot.

The dinner itself was a huge success, thank goodness. With entertainment by singers Nancy Wilson and Billy Ecksteine, humor by Dick Gregory and Bill Cosby, and an electrifying speech by actor/orator Ossie Davis. Mr. Davis told the mesmerized audience that "It's not the man; It's the plan. It's not the rap; it's the map."

In Mr. Davis's remarks, he said, "And that's why tonight, the burden of my appeal to you, to the 13

---

[56] The dinner was held on June 18, 1971.

Congressional Black Caucus members, to give up a plan of action. Give to us a '10 Black commandments,' simple, strong, that we can carry in our hearts, and in our memories no matter where we are and reach out and touch and feel the reassurance that there is behind everything we do a simple, moral, intelligent plan that must be fulfilled in the course of time even if all of our leaders one by one, fall in the battle (and feel the reassurance that there is behind everything we do a simple, moral, intelligent plan that must be fulfilled in the course of time. Even if all of our leaders one by one, fall in the battle). Somebody will rise and say, Brother, 'Our leader died while we're on page 3 of a plan, now that the funeral is over, let us proceed to page 4."[57]

Another excerpt of Mr. Davis' remarks: "At the time Dr. King died in 1968, he was in the process of organizing his forces and calling upon his people to come one more time to Washington, D.C. And I have a feeling that he had come that time he would not have said, "I have a dream." He would have said, "I have a plan." And I feel that that plan he had might have made the difference."[58]

---

[57] Mr. Davis's speech can be found in *Ossie Davis, Life Lit by Some Large Vision: Selected Speeches and Writings*, (New York: Atria Books, 2006), pp. 25–26. In parenthesis are edits to reflect the speech as written in Davis's book.

[58] Ibid.

Randall Robinson and Robert Johnson Recent Graduates

After Randall Robinson finished Harvard University Law School, he called, and I arranged for him to work for Rep. Charles Diggs, Jr. in the area of African Affairs, beginning of his subsequent, celebrated career as the founder/president of TransAfrica.[59]

Robert Johnson, after he graduated with a master's degree in international relations from Princeton, called about working in Washington, D.C. I knew that Sterling Tucker, President of Washington Urban League, was looking for a PR director. I referred Bob to Sterling, who hired him. A year later, Bob Johnson called about working on Capitol Hill. I knew that Delano Lewis, as Chief of Staff for Rep. Walter Fauntroy, was looking for a press secretary and I referred Bob to Delano, and he was hired. Bob later went to work for the National

---

[59] "In 1977, he founded TransAfrica—a lobbying group dedicated to promoting "enlightened and progressive" U.S. foreign policy toward countries in Africa and the Caribbean. As president of TransAfrica, Robinson led the U.S. campaign to bring democracy to South Africa, putting an end to that county's apartheid policies." Retrieved on May 28, 2017 at http://biography.yourdictionary.com/randall-robinson#X8guOp8bfpufoVV7.99

Cable TV Association. From there he became founder of BET. And the rest is history.

Robert Johnson once stated: "Ofield Dukes is a brilliant PR strategist, well connected and was very helpful to me in the beginning of my career."

LeBaron Taylor, a former Detroiter, a Pioneer in the Promotion of Black Music

LeBaron Taylor, as Vice President of CBS Records and later as Vice President of Sony Music Entertainment, was not only a client but a most loyal friend. I became his closest advisor and got his company involved with the National Urban Coalition, the Congressional Black Caucus, among others. He and Sony for years sponsored the most elegant event at the Congressional Black Caucus Annual Legislative Conference, "The LaGrande Affaire." He was an early organizer of recorded Black music and Black Music Month. He called regularly to always thank me for my support and for being his friend.

His sudden death from cancer was a shock, even to his wife, Dr. Kay Lovelace Taylor. On September 13, 2000, I coordinated and served as executive producer of a Musical Tribute to LeBaron Taylor at the Warner Theatre in Washington raising $38,000 for the LeBaron Taylor Scholarship Fund. Entertainers included Jerry Butler, Peabo Bryson,

Henny Lattimore, Regina Belle, Jean Carne, Carl Anderson, and Cheryl Lynn. LeBaron Taylor was a very prominent but an unsung hero in the recording industry and my best friend.

Exciting Trip to Africa Sweden

In my 10-day trip to Sweden in October, 1971, I was a guest of the Swedish government and had the unique opportunity of meeting with Dr. Gunnar Myrdal, the author of the epic book on American race relations, "The American Dilemma," as well as meet with the president of Sweden and the president of the Swedish parliament. Arrangements were made for me to spend a weekend in Uppsala, the ski country where I had a rendezvous with my girlfriend who was on teaching assignment in Europe.

Inauguration of Detroit's First Black Mayor— Coleman Young

In 1973, I was called by two aides to Detroit's newly elected first Black mayor, William "Bill" Beckham and Malcolm Dade, about returning to Detroit after Thanksgiving to help organize a meaningful inauguration for Mayor Coleman Young, who, like me, was a product of Detroit's Black Bottom.[60]

I returned to Detroit and outlined a three-day inauguration with 12 different committees, involving 100 committee members. There were those who questioned my being asked to come from Washington, D.C. to do this, because they thought there were those in Detroit who could do it better. However, I did have the experience of working on the inaugural committee of President Johnson in 1965.

In Detroit, the three-day inauguration in January 1974, called for an initial prayer breakfast, a business-labor luncheon, an inaugural concert featuring Diana Ross, major youth and senior citizen activities, a special pre-inaugural ball reception for Detroit elite society and business community, and a climaxing inaugural ball. I considered myself smart by having a special committee of media, representing television, radio, and newspapers, assisting in arranging the best possible logistics for covering the inauguration.

---

[60] Coleman Young was elected as Detroit's first Black mayor in 1973. William Beckham served as deputy mayor and Malcolm Dade was a Detroit political strategist.

The prayer breakfast was ecumenical with the catholic cardinal, Jewish rabbi and top protestant leadership, attended by more than 3,000.[61]

The business-labor luncheon was historic, attended by the presidents of the four automobile companies, the president of the UAW and the Republican governor[62]. This made national news. A sellout crowd of close to 4,000 attended.

At the inaugural concert, in spite of eight inches of snow, a capacity crowd of about 4,000 joined Diana Ross as she sat on the stage of the Masonic Theatre and had the entire audience to reach out and touch somebody, as she sang.

Detroit's white society and white business heavy hitters attended the glitzy, red carpet pre-inaugural ball reception, co-chaired by Esther Gordy Edwards, Vice President of Motown, and Lanie Pincus, the wife of Max Pincus, the president of a major Detroit men's retail store, Hughes & Hatcher.

---

[61] According to the *Chicago Tribune* article, "The mayor who knows his people," the breakfast had an "audience of 3,000 who had paid $5 for a scrambled egg and sausage breakfast at Coo Hall, shouted 'amen' and 'right on.'" Retrieved from http://archives.chicagotribune.com/1974/01/09/page/14/article/the-mayor-who-knows-his-people

[62] William G. Milliken served as governor between 1969–1982.

An hour or so before the 10 a.m. starting time of the inaugural ball, I received a call from a Black militant group from Detroit's east side threatening to "turn the mother_____ out" if they were not given free tickets to the ball. My quick response was, "Brother, how many tickets do you need?"

Ten thousand people attended the inaugural ball.[63] The attendees celebrated the historic occasion in grand style. And, thank God, there were no incidents.

The media coverage was tremendous. The daily newspapers, TV and radio stations described the inauguration in glowing terms as a "new renaissance" in Detroit in the election of its first Black mayor.

About the inauguration, the *Detroit Free Press* wrote in a December 12, 1973 article:

> Henry Ford II and Leonard Woodcock (president of the UAW) will share a podium, Diana Ross and the Detroit Sympathy Orchestra will share the stage and Mayor-Elect Coleman Young will try to see the inaugural with more than 25,000 Detroiters in the biggest celebration of its kind ever

---

[63] The *Chicago Tribune* reported in the article, "The mayor who knows his people," that "at the inaugural ball a crowd of at least 8,000 showed up to salute 'our mayor,' even the only 5,000 tickets had been printed and not more than 3,000 persons were expected." Retrieved from http://archives.chicagotribune.com/1974/01/09/page/14/article/the-mayor-who-knows-his-people

attempted here. Plans for three days of festivities were formally unveiled yesterday as more than 100 volunteer workers on Young's different inaugural committees met in the Sheraton Cadillac Hotel.

Ofield Dukes, coordinator for the inaugural committee, said Young is making arrangements to include several hundred low-income persons, students and disabled veterans in the events as his guests.

For my efforts, I was nominated for and won the "Oscar" of public relations, the Public Relations Society's competitive Silver Anvil.[64]

Other Early Public Recognition

In 1976, the *Washington Post* magazine section, The Potomac, did a front-page feature on the top six public relations persuaders in the nation's capital. I was, surprisingly, included in that special feature.[65]

---

[64] "Detroit inaugural group wins Silver Anvil Award," original report can be found at:
https://books.google.com/books?id=uo8DAAAAMBAJ&pg=PA50 &lpg=PA50&dq=silver+anvil+awards+Ofield+Dukes&source=bl&ot s=JZ1PuCRRSN&sig=LHtXGL2_m-30qGOjh9dg7rhipGo&hl=zh-CN&sa=X&ved=oahUKEwj62sq3rrPSAhVEoYMKHT_iBpAQ6 AEIVDAH#v=onepage&q=silver%20anvil%20awards%20Ofield %20Dukes&f=false

[65] Ruby Maxa, "Six Persuaders: Have They Got PR for You," *The Washington Post*, March 10, 1974. Retrieved from https://search.proquest.com/docview/146196283?accountid=14214

This was a tremendous benefit to my professional stature and credibility as a Black public relations practitioner operating in the mainstream of public relations.

Beginning Teaching Career at Howard University's School of Communications

In 1971, I was recruited by my good friend from Detroit, Tony Brown, serving as the first dean of Howard University's School of Communications, to teach the first courses in public relations at Howard. This was an exciting challenge. I began teaching two courses, introduction to public relations and an advanced course in public relations. The initial interest in this new profession by Howard students was overwhelming. I had an average of 40 students crowding in my class, with a normal maximum of 25. I turned the advanced class into an internship.

In my class, I was very stern. The students had to assume the study of PR as a job. They had to attend class on time, or after a 10-minute period, the class doors were locked. They had to dress appropriately. A major focus was on the philosophy of Dr. William James and would tell my class paraphrasing James saying the "greatest discovery of the 20th Century was that one's attitude determined how far you go in life." So, my first challenge was dealing with the attitudes of my students, stressing having a passion for excellence, being not good writers but excellent, developing a strong work ethic, forgoing any excuses about their race, having an intense desire and determination to overcome any obstacles, racial or otherwise, in their path. The importance of following Socrates' advice of knowing who they are, having a deep understanding and taking pride in who they are and in their race; having high confidence and self-esteem, practicing the three "C's": confidence, competence and competitiveness.

I had my students to greet each other warmly, with a smile, with positive comments, as to promote better inter-personal communications. We also had students to call their parents to tell them they loved them, to send birthday notes/cards to grandparents, relatives, and friends, to actively engage in the practice of public relations, not just as students learning the principles, tools and techniques of public relations. The emphasis was on Dale Carnegie's PR bible of "How to Win Friends and Influence People," and the golden rule of treating others as you would want to be treated.

We placed great emphasis on the fact that each student had a self-image and a public image and the self-image reflected a mental picture of "the kind of person we think we are." And the public image is what we want to project to others and for others to perceive of us. Also, students need to work very hard to improve their attitude about who they are and how to achieve the essential character traits to project a positive public image.

I had all my students to go through a written self-evaluation of the following traits, which, I suggested made up an outstanding public relations practitioner: integrity, honesty, objectivity (not influenced by prejudices, limitations of own experiences, perceptions), attitude-positive or negative, optimism or pessimism, tact/diplomacy/sensitivity, trustworthiness, loyalty, resourcefulness/persistence, creativity, time management/punctuality, self-esteem/self-confidence, humility versus egotism, dependability, self-motivation/self-initiative, sense of humor, perceptive/insightful, and calm demeanor.

Since I had the opportunity of working with one of the great public relations practitioners in American history, President Lyndon B. Johnson, I shared with my students his Ten Public Relations Principles:

1. Become an effective listener. Learn to remember names. Inefficiency at this point may indicate that your interest is not sufficiently outgoing.

2. Be a comfortable person to those individuals so they don't feel a strain while in your presence.

3. Acquire the quality of a relaxed, easy-going manner, so that things do not ruffle you.

4. Don't be egotistical. Guard against the impression that you know it all.

5. Cultivate the quality of being interesting so people will get something of value from their association with you.

6. Study to eliminate the "scratchy" elements out of your personality, even those of which you may be unaware.

7. Sincerely attempt to heal, on an honest Christian basis, every misunderstanding you have had or will have in the future.

8. Practice liking people until you learn to do so genuinely.

9. Never miss an opportunity to say a word of congratulations upon one's achievements or express sympathy in sorrow or disappointment.

10. Give spiritual strength to people and they will give genuine affection to you.

The first part of each class dealt with current events, challenging the students, intellectually, of being aware of those critical events happening in our country and in other parts of the world. My point was intelligence is not solely based on the accumulation of information from a textbook but the knowledge of what is happening in their world. I said some cab drivers, who had observed the coming and going of American presidents and other history makers, were more knowledgeable than many Ph.D. graduates.

Another important emphasis in my class was not allowing anyone to leave without outlining on paper a five-year career vision of what they wanted to do in life. I referred to the remarks of Dr. Benjamin Mays, then the president of Morehouse College, who emphasized that the greatest sin in life is not achieving your dream; the greatest sin in life is not having a dream to achieve.[66]

For the advanced PR class, based on my contacts, I arranged for the students to have internships at the U.S. Department of Labor, the National Education Association, in the office of Congressional Black Caucus members, at my office, and at the White House, CIA, among others.

One of my students who became one of the first Blacks to work as an intern at the National Education Association was almost fired for not reporting to work. I had a long conversation with her

---

[66] Specifically, Benjamin E. Mays said, "The tragedy of life doesn't lie in not reaching your goal. The tragedy lies in having no goal to reach. It isn't a calamity to die with dreams unfulfilled, but it is a calamity not to dream. It is not a disgrace not to reach the stars, but it is a disgrace to have no stars to reach for, not failure, but low aim, is sin." As quoted in http://crim.education.gsu.edu/aboutus/dr-benjamin-e-mays/

about dependability. She returned, was a dedicated intern, and after graduation ended up working on the public relations staff of Oprah Winfrey. She, Robin Beaman, now operates a successful PR firm in Chicago.

Emergence of Cathy Hughes and Her Radio Career

When Cathy Hughes was manager of Howard University's popular WHUR Radio, she was challenged almost daily by Retired General Frederic Davison, as a chief advisor to Howard University President Dr. James Cheek. Cathy was calling me almost every day in distress for comfort and advice. In June, 1977, I arranged for a top lawyer in Washington, the most eloquent Atty. Belford Lawson, Jr. to handle her case. He filed a lawsuit that she won.

In an article in the Afro-American newspaper, the headline read: "Female Manager of WHUR Files $100,000 suit." The article read, "Catherine E. Liggins, general manager of WHUR-FM, is seeking $100,000 in damages from retired Major General Frederic Davison. The suit, filed in District Court last week by Belford V. Lawson, Jr., attorney, contends that Davison had subjected Mrs. Liggins to 'severe harassment, intimidation, verbal abuse, discrimination, insults, foul language and threats.'"

Davison was serving as the Executive Assistant to Howard University President, Dr. James Cheek. Cathy won her case.

Later, when Cathy was ready to enter radio ownership, my wife, Rosa, and I purchased stock and I raised an additional $100,000 for her to buy at depressed market value, WOL-AM Radio.

At the 25th anniversary of WOL and Radio One, Cathy attributed her success to my support and assistance, saying "I was a diamond in the rough and Ofield Dukes added the polish to contribute to my success. Ofield Dukes not only invested in the purchase of the first radio station but also recruited other investors. He was one of the first persons to have faith in me."

XIII.

Democratic Party Presidential and Congressional Involvement

Behind my deep involvement in the 1968 presidential campaign as a member of the campaign staff of Democratic presidential candidate, Hubert H. Humphrey, I begin in 1972 attending every Democratic National Convention and became more active in Democratic politics. I worked in the Democratic presidential campaigns of 1972, 1976, 1980, 1984, 1988, 1992, 1996, 2000 and 2004.

In 1986, I worked as a strategist very closely with Dr. C. Delores Tucker. She was chair of the DNC Black Caucus, and I helped mobilize Black voter support that led to Democrats winning U.S. Senate races in 10 states and regaining control of the senate to prevent President Ronald Reagan from adding conservatives to the U.S. Supreme Court.

In 1988, C. Delores, again as Chair of the DNC Black Caucus, convened a meeting in Atlanta of Black Democratic leaders with DNC Chair Paul Kirk out of concern for the lack of Black consultants at DNC and limited Black participation at

Democratic National Convections. More than 30
Black leaders and Democratic strategists from
throughout the country attended the meeting. That
was the great influence of C. Delores Tucker.

Mr. Kirk responded to the political pressure by
agreeing to make changes at the national convention
in Atlanta especially in light of increased minority
interest in the presidential candidacy of Rev. Jesse L.
Jackson, Sr.

A main result of the meeting was my firm being
hired to work with DNC Communications Director,
Michael McCurry, to organize for the first time a
plan to facilitate minority media coverage of the
convention in Atlanta.

We ended up with record participation of Black
media representatives in the convention and other
minority media representatives and exceptional
coverage in African-American newspapers and on
radio stations.

Also, implemented for the first time at a
Democratic National Convention was an affirmative
action program to increase the number of Black
vendors.

The great success of minority media
participation in the Atlanta convention resulted in
my serving as a paid communications consultant to
subsequent DNC chairpersons and as coordinator of

Specialty Media at every Democratic convention from 1988 to 2004.

I worked very closely with DNC Chairman Ronald (Ron) Brown, the first Black chairman of the Democratic Party, in the 1992 election of Bill Clinton and his re-election in 1996.

I remember on one occasion Ron calling me about his travels throughout the country in 1992 and finding, in his words, "the brothers and sisters not knowing what I am doing." I did a special article for the more than 200 Black papers describing how Brown was laying the foundation for his "Mission Possible" of electing a Democrat as president. At Brown's funeral in 1996, President Clinton said the obvious, if it had not been for the Black vote and Brown's leadership, he would not have been elected president in 1992 and re-elected in 1996.

The Ice-T/Time Warner Crisis

At the 1992, Democratic National Convention in New York City, I was confronted with an expected but most interesting and challenging client problem. Tom Draper, Vice President of Time Warner Inc., called me urgently. One of the company's recording stars, Ice-T, had recorded a highly popular but controversial record bragging about killing cops.[67]

The Time Warner board of trustees and top management of the company were quite upset about the negative publicity from the recording. Draper asked me to meet with Ms. Sylvia Rhone, Chair and CEO of the ATCO/EastWest Recording Company. Her office was in New York City. In our meeting, she asked me to develop a report in response to the controversy for her presentation to the Time Warner board of directors.

In between my duties at the Democratic National Convention as Specialty Media Coordinator, I began work on the project. I contacted a former student who was in the recording business in New York and asked her to do research on rap music and its cultural and financial impact on the music market.

I, within a week, developed a fairly comprehensive report on the history of rap music, its culture and economic benefits to rap musicians. We described rap music as the language of what some Black sociologists have called the "Black underclass," of the frustrations and disillusionment of problem-plagued young Black males, of the inner city, of young people, unemployed, underemployed, of the

---

[67] Ice-T signed to Warner Bros. Sire Records.

unskilled, living in the long dark shadows of an economic depression.

I added that "There are those who feel Time Warner has a corporate citizenship responsibility to hear and understand the language of the rappers, and seek to address the problems conveyed by the messengers. And there are still others, especially some African-American leaders, who feel that Time Warner has and continues to enjoy the profits from rap artists and remain allegedly insensitive to the messages and of the rap messengers."

I indicated in the report that on the Billboard Rhythm and Blues (R&B) chart, 40 percent of the top 100 recordings, based on retail sales, were rap recordings. Of the Billboard top 200 albums, based on retail sales, approximately 15 percent was rap. I added that when we look at the demographics of the rap music market, increasingly the main consumers and purchasers of rap music albums and records were very wide spread, geographically, ethnically, economically and racially, crossing all boundaries. Among the present heavy purchasers were upper-income, suburban white teenagers.

Ms. Rhone made her report to the Time Warner board and her report was accepted. My client, Tom Draper and Ms. Rhone, were most pleased. So was I.

Back to Democratic politics, in 1998, I worked with the DNC and Rep. Charles Rangel in helping to develop and implement a communication strategy to educate and energize Black voters that resulted in a heavy Black voter turnout and Democratic victories that changed the political landscape in the nation's capital.

In 2000, I served as a communications consultant in the presidential campaign of Gore-Lieberman, working with campaign manager Donna Brazile.

Tribute to Ronald Brown, First Black Chairman of the Democratic National Committee

After serving as chairman of Rev. Jesse Jackson's 1988 presidential campaign, Ronald Brown explored the notion of running for chairman of the Democratic National Committee.

Politics was his heart and Ron Brown's political impact on America, as the first Black chairman of a national political party, would be unprecedented and immeasurable.

In an April 18, 1996 article on the tragic death of Brown, I wrote: "When Brown ran for chairman of the Democratic Party in 1989 of a divided and depressed Democratic party that had suffered a smashing defeat in the 1988 presidential election, many of his friends were skeptical of his chances of winning and even more pessimistic about his being able to pull off a miracle by resurrecting and revitalizing a moribund Democratic Party."

The article continued: "Although President George Bush was riding high with a huge public popularity rating, DNC Chairman Brown traveled throughout the county revamping the Party's campaign operation, working diligently as a diplomat extraordinaire in bringing the warring factions of the Party together, attracting needed finances, and preaching a strange doctrine—the Democrats could recapture the White House."

"And thanks to Brown's genius for both details and consensus building, Bill Clinton won the White House in 1992 and was re-elected in 1996." I had the unique opportunity of working with Brown in 1992 and again in 1996 as a communications consultant to the Democratic National Committee.

In his eulogy at Brown's funeral, President Clinton said that had it not been for Ron Brown, he would not be in this job today.[68]

---

[68] The original text of William Jefferson Clinton's remarks at the Funeral of Secretary of Commerce Ronald H. Brown, April 10, 1996 stated: "On a personal note, I want to say to my friend just one last time: Thank you; if it weren't for you, I wouldn't be here." The quote can be found at http://www.presidency.ucsb.edu/ws/?pid=52653

XIV.

Passage of D.C. Home Rule

In 1973, Rep. Charles C. Diggs, Jr., as the first Black chairman of the United States House Committee on the District of Columbia in the 165-year history of the District of Columbia, called during the congressional debate on the D.C. Home Rule bill. He said some members of congress felt District residents were complacent about Home Rule. I was asked to work with local leadership in mobilizing public support for the bill, which would provide District residents with limited self-government.

I called Ms. Flaxie Pinkett, President of John R. Pinkett, Inc. (a real estate and insurance firm) and an influential leader in the city, who became co-chair of the home-rule effort.[69] She and several other prominent D.C. leaders and elected officials worked hard for the support of the bill. Rep. Diggs was able

---

[69] Flaxie Madison Pinkett was an activist, a social entrepreneur, and a dynamic African-American woman. She inherited John R. Pinkett, Inc.; the first insurance and real estate firm in Washington, D.C. that was fully owned and operated by an African American. http://www.wdchumanities.org/dcdm/exhibits/show/flaxie

to get tremendous support for the bill in its passage
in the House by a vote of 343 to 74. Rep. Diggs also
pushed through the congress the bill establishing the
University of the District of Columbia.

Rep. Diggs has received little recognition for his
history-making efforts on behalf of the District of
Columbia.

Inauguration of D.C.'s First Elected Government in 100 years

Mayor-elect Walter Washington called and
invited my firm to organize and coordinate a three-
day inauguration for those elected to city
government after the passage of the D.C. Home Rule
bill. This was significant history, the first elected
D.C. government in 100 years.

We went to work and organized a first-class
committee of dozens, and on January 2–5, 1975,
inaugural events were held for the Mayor, chairman
and members of the D.C. City Council. A theme of
the inauguration was "Washington, D.C. A City Re-
Born." Thousands of proud and excited D.C.
residents participated in the three-day inauguration.

Mayor Marion Barry's Kitchen Cabinet

In the first mayoral term of Marion Barry, he formed a "Kitchen Cabinet" of advisors that consisted of Delano Lewis, president of the C&P Telephone Company, Robert Johnson, president of Black Entertainment Television, David Abramson, president of his advertising company (Abramson Ehrlich Manes), and me.[70]

We often had meetings at the office of Delano Lewis or at my office at the National Press Building. During that period, Mayor Barry was an attentive listener and was responsive to our advice.

I advised him to stop wearing his dashiki every day presumably (he wore it) to identify with his native Africa. I told him he was now the mayor of the residents of the District of Columbia, and his daily attire should represent the wear of his constituents. He did not have to be different.

Also, at the time, Mayor Barry became involved in a public shouting match with conservative Republican Congressman of Virginia, Joel Broyhill. I was able to convince Mayor Barry to go visit Rep. Broyhill in his office and "kill" him with kindness. And Mayor Barry did that and as a result had a more productive relationship with Rep. Broyhill.

---

[70] Marion Barry's first term began in 1979.

In addition, I chaired a VIP public relations committee to develop and promote a most positive image for the District. We also re-organized the city government's communications operation and established the office of press secretary for the mayor.

Mayor Barry expressed great satisfaction for the early support of his "Kitchen Cabinet" during the challenges of his first term in office.

XV.

ODA National and International Projects

Among the national projects that I had the opportunity to participate in included the following: Joint Center for Political Studies, Operation Big Vote, March to establish the Martin Luther King, Jr. Holiday, and South Africa Visit.

Founding of the Joint Center for Political Studies and Operation Big Vote

One of the significant political development in 1972 was the founding of The Joint Center for Political and Economic Studies, inspired by the leadership of Louis Martin, Frank Reeves, and Dr. Kenneth B. Clark. I was called upon to handle the early public relations in the founding of the Joint Center.

A key person in the growth, development and national impact of the Joint Center was Eddie Williams, as the founding president of the Joint Center. He made the Joint Center a nationally prominent Black think tank patterned after Brookings, Aspen Institute, and the Urban Institute.

The Joint Center is still recognized as "The Black Think Tank" that focuses on political, economic and other public policy issues of greatest concern to African Americans. This was due to the leadership of Eddie Williams who served as president of the Joint Center for 32 years.

In addition to being president of the Joint Center, Williams was simultaneously the founding board chairman of the National Coalition on Black Voter Participation, founded by civil rights leaders in 1976. I served as a founding board member of the Coalition, which is now formally known as the National Coalition on Black Civic Participation.

Eddie Williams provided essential national leadership in the national political impact of the Joint Center and Coalition on Black Voter Participation.

Stevie Wonder March to Make Dr. Martin Luther King's Birthday a National Holiday

In 1981, I received a call from Stevie Wonder and his manager, Ewart Abner, about my firm organizing an event in Washington, D.C. to promote public attention on legislation introduced by Detroit

Congressman John Conyers, Jr. to make Dr. Martin Luther King's birthday a national holiday.

I agreed to accept the challenge. I organized an extensive committee and begin planning a national march on Washington, D.C. for January 1981.

We began a national outreach to Black disc jockeys at radio stations throughout the country and civil rights organizations. We instituted a national media campaign. The march would be in front of the U.S. Capitol.

Stevie recorded a song that was high on the record chart, "Happy Birthday to You." He was an important factor in publicizing the march in media interviews. Stevie would drop by my office at the National Press Building, unannounced to chat about plans and logistics for the march. He had invited Diana Ross and other special guests. And there were some prominent people, one person in particular that he was not receptive to having on the program. I will not mention any names.

Dealing with the logistics of hundreds of buses bringing people to Washington for the march was a major challenge. Where would they park? What food and other facilities would be available to them? What would be traffic and crowd control? I recruited the best officials in Washington to work with the D.C. Police and Capitol Hill and National Park Police on these logistics and problems.

It was four a.m. the morning of the march, and I was in my office, as it began to snow. The calls were coming in from the different delegations of people traveling by chartered buses, by Greyhound buses, train, by airplane, by cars for the mid-day march. It turned out to be a cold January day. But disc jockeys from throughout the country had responded, including Tom Joyner from Indiana.

More than 100,000 people showed up on that cold, snowy, but historic day to support the Stevie Wonder march to make Dr. King's birthday a national holiday. After the march, Stevie hosted a concert at the Capital Centre for 18,000 attendees, including Mrs. Coretta Scott King and members of the King family.

From the march, we launched a national petition campaign with thousands of petitions to be presented to members of the U.S. Congress in support of that legislation.

One published reaction to the march was this:

> Good Gods of People—that was activist Dick Gregory's description of the more than 100,000 persons who braved the snow and cold weather for the Stevie Wonder March. More than 300 buses brought the marchers from about 30 cities. The white media in Washington initially downgrade the crowd estimate to 10,000, which was called 'ridiculous' by March participants. Rev. Jesse

Jackson, Rep. Walter Fauntroy, and Gregory, who participated in the 1963 March on Washington, estimated the crowd at more than 200,000.

At the time, I was a member of the board of directors of the Martin Luther King, Jr. Center for Non-Violent Social Change.

A Scary Moment Involving Mrs. Richard Nixon And Stevie Wonder

One of my summertime activities was supporting entertainment activities, special concerts, on the mall. Since Motown was a client, in this instance I had the responsibility for coordinating Stevie Wonder's highly publicized concert on the mall near the Washington Monument.

For this concert, the Nixon White House arranged for Mrs. Richard Nixon to be a special guest.

This was an unusual event for Mrs. Nixon, not known whether she was a Stevie Wonder fan or was there out of curiosity or for public relations reasons. Possibly the think was she would be there to say hello to Stevie, take a quick photo and be gone. Anyway, she was there with an array of secret service agents and a crowd of more than 10,000 ardent Stevie Wonder fans.

Stevie was due from Baltimore. However, for whatever reason, he had not arrived at 4 p.m., the announced time for the concert. But Mrs. Nixon was there sitting on the stage. At 4:15 p.m., still no Stevie Wonder. The crowd was becoming somewhat anxious. And so were the secret service agents.

At 4:30 p.m., still no word from Stevie Wonder. I, too, became anxious. The secret service agents conferred with me. Mrs. Nixon seemed nervous on stage as the crowd began to chant, "Where is Stevie? Where is Stevie?" I did not have an answer. There was realistic concern about the crowd becoming boisterous and uncontrollable. The agents had obvious concern about Mrs. Nixon's safety.

Agents surrounded her on the stage, as she squirmed nervously on the stage.

There suddenly came cheers from the crowd, as Stevie Wonder arrived at about 4:45 p.m. As Stevie approached the stage, he was greeted by Mrs. Nixon who grabbed and hugged him. That was the news photo of the day, Mrs. Richard Nixon hugging Motown star Stevie Wonder. But the photo caption did not capture the actual moment of Mrs. Nixon hugging Stevie out of great relief that he had arrived and she was safe from possibly being mobbed by the huge gathering of Stevie Wonder fans if he failed to show.

That was a scary scene.

International Project—Human Rights—South Africa—A Public Relations Dilemma

Mrs. Coretta Scott King's 10-day visit to South Africa for the Enthronement of Desmond Mpilo Tutu as the Eleventh Lord Archbishop of Cape Town, South Africa and a possible visit with South African President, P.W. Botha, prior to the end of apartheid.

In 1986, as a member of her board, I was invited by Mrs. King to be a member of her entourage to South Africa, serving as her press person and media spokesperson. This was an extraordinary trip with aspects of controversy. Anti-forces of apartheid were still fighting that racially oppressive system and had their own concerns about Mrs. King being invited to the country by South African President P.W. Botha. Mr. Botha had to approved visas for her delegation and extensive use of South African police for her security.

Our first stop in Africa was in Harare, Zimbabwe for an international conference of non-aligned nations. Mrs. King invited me to join her in a series of meetings with the presidents of African countries. From there we traveled to Johannesburg, where Mrs. King and our delegation met with South African leaders and others involved in the anti-apartheid movement. We spent two days in Johannesburg.

We then went to Cape Town, a major highlight of our South African journey, for the historic enthronement of Archbishop Tutu. This would be the beautiful scene of our triumph and the backdrop of what amounted to a near political disaster.

The day after Archbishop Tutu's enthronement as the new Lord Archbishop of the Episcopal Church in Cape Town, a seething controversy developed over Mrs. King's pending meeting with South African President P.W. Botha. Mrs. King had a heart-warming visit at the home of Winnie Mandela in Soweto and was the VIP guest of Lord Archbishop Tutu in Cape Town. However, both Lord Archbishop Tutu and Mrs. Mandela, joined by militant apartheid foe, Allan Boesak, were in strong, public opposition to Mrs. King meeting with President Botha.

With a huge international media and all media in South African covering Mrs. King's visit, the conflict became front-page news in South Africa and major news throughout the United States and the world.

After extensive pressure from Archbishop Tutu, Mrs. Mandela and Rev. Boesak, Mrs. King had to reconsider her meeting with P.W. Botha. One newspaper headline read: "Boesak says he won't meet Coretta King."

The pressure and negative press bothered Mrs. King. This was an unexpected crisis in her visit to South Africa. What were her alternatives for resolving what has become an international embarrassment?

That evening, Mrs. King convened a mid-night meeting of her staff of advisors. There was some discussion of quietly returning to the States.

During the discussion, I suggested sending a letter to Mr. Botha not cancelling, but postponing the meeting. Mrs. King asked me to draft such a letter, have it typed the first thing in the morning. She indicated that she was scheduled to have breakfast with a top advisor to Mr. Botha. She would give him the letter to pass on to Mr. Botha.

Early the next morning, I drafted a brief letter, had problems finding an American typewriter for typing the letter. I finally did, and gave the letter to Mrs. King who asked the advisor to Mr. Botha to give it to him as soon as possible. That was about 9 a.m. At 9:30 a.m., Mrs. King began a series of calls to Mr. Botha's office to check on his receipt of her letter. She was not getting through. Almost every half hour, calls were made to President Botha's office, still no definitive response. Her meeting with Mr. Botha was scheduled for 12:30 p.m.

By noon, reportedly a large gathering of media had assembled in the courtyard adjacent to Mr. Botha's office. Mrs. King and all of us became concerned about not receiving any word from Mr. Botha about the receipt of Mrs. King's letter and the status of the 12:30 p.m. meeting.

According to reports, at about 12:15, Mr. Botha strolled out to the courtyard and mingled with the media representatives and indicated that he was waiting to meet with Mrs. King. At 12:30 p.m., the meeting time, reportedly Mr. Botha expressed surprise that Mrs. King had not arrived for the meeting. Ten or 15 minutes later, he announced that he had been snubbed by Mrs. King. And the South African and international media ran with that sensational story

The *Cape Time* headline read: "Storm Follows Snub by King." The article read in part, "A political storm has engulfed Mrs. Coretta Scott King after the visiting American civil rights leader yesterday buckled to United Democratic Front pressures by ducking out of a pre-arranged meeting with 'establishment' leaders such as President P.W. Botha and Chief Mangosuthu Buthelezi."

Mrs. King was so irritated at the public pressure and role of Rev. Boesak that when he showed up at her hotel the next day, she refused to see him. As her press spokesman, Mrs. King asked me to meet with the horde of media representatives to explain what really happened. Archbishop Tutu, Mrs. Mandela and Rev. Boesak also vehemently opposed Mrs. King meeting with Zulu Chief Mangosuthu Buthelezi, leader of South Africa's six million Zulus, whose "moderate" views were opposed by Mrs. Mandela and Rev. Boesak, according to a Reuter's article that appeared in *The Washington Times*.[71]

I was quoted in the same article as saying Mrs. King's trip was "a tremendous success and that Mrs. King would brief Secretary of State George Shultz on her return home and would be happy to pass on her impressions to President Ronald Reagan."

Later in the day, Mrs. King did meet with Rev. Boesak, had a 30-minute conversation with him and then met with reporters. Rev. Boesak commended Mrs. King as "wise and courageous" in her last-minute decision not to keep her appointment with President Botha.

When we returned to Washington, I sent a long letter to *Washington Post* columnist Bill Raspberry who wrote that it was a mistake for Mrs. King to

---

[71] According to the Joshua Project, an estimated 13 million Zulu people exist in 2017. https://joshuaproject.net/people_groups/16112

engage in such foreign matters.[72] Bill had his facts
mixed up, as did most other reporters. The lesson we learned is that P.W. Botha was mischievously shrewd in manipulating the media to suit his own interests. A second lesson is not putting a lot of trust in so-called friends and allies, who are subject to betray you based on their own interests. Prior to leaving America, Mrs. King tried reaching Rev. Bosesak for a general conversation, but he reportedly was not available. The good news is that the South African trip did not tarnish Mrs. King's image or reputation.

Alex Haley and Roots—*20ᵗʰ Century Drama, History and Triumph*

In 1971, George Haley, brother of Alex Haley, called about Alex needing office space to finish writing his epic book, *Roots*. Alex had been pursuing this mission for a number of years, speaking around the country about the origin of our roots to stay economically afloat.

---

[72] This comment comes from Bill Raspberry's article "Coretta King Needed Better 'Road Map' Of South Africa", published on September 16, 1986. The article available at: http://articles.sun-sentinel.com/1986-09-16/news/8602240842_1_botha-coretta-scott-king-africa

I agreed to sublet one room of my office at the National Press Building for Alex, with Alex actually signing a sub-lease agreement with me and the management of the Press Building. If he failed to pay, I, as the main tenant, was responsible.

For several years, Alex would work, sometimes all night, at his Underwood typewriter, supported by his researcher and secretary. He was a compulsive worker. All he had in the room was a desk, an Underwood typewriter and a couch with all of his research material. Sometimes he would work for days and nights on end, stopping only for a few hours to sleep on the couch. I would come in the morning and find him perspiring and still writing.

There came a point of economic crisis for Alex. Doubleday had cancelled his credit card, because he was twelve years behind on the publication date and up to his ears in debt.

Alex also expressed the painful pressure of trying to finish the last chapters of *Roots*. He said something was missing. He was not certain of what, but he needed to empathize with the thousands of African slaves, on the dirty, dingy, smelly slave boats bringing them to new shores of enslavement.

So, he decided on a final trip to Africa to try to relive that frightful experience. Upon his return, he confided in me that on a dark, lonely, forlorn night on the ship returning to America, he was depressed;

standing there in the pitch darkness. For a moment, he said he thought of ending it. But as he leaned over the railing of the ship, with the thought of jumping in a black, watery grave, he said he suddenly heard a voice, and he recognized the voice. It was his Aunt Kizzy. And she was saying to Alex, "Alex, you can do it. Alex, you can do it. Alex, you can do it."

Alex said he heard her voice. In a moment of sheer encouragement, he ran to the belly of the ship, took off his clothes, and he said he finally got the feeling, he finally felt the pain and sorrow of the slaves in their sordid misery. He finally got the feeling. Now, he could finish *Roots*.

In the meantime, Alex was falling behind in his obligated rent to the Press Building. Upon his return to the States, he went to Trinidad to finish writing. After receiving a handwritten letter from him, I sent him a promissory note to sign, promising the Press Club he would take care of the back debt in a specified period of time. Alex, returned the promissory note, unsigned, along with a handwritten note that he was working on the final chapter of *Roots*.

A couple of weeks later, Bernard Morris, manager of the Press Building, came by my office on a Friday afternoon. He said, "Mr. Dukes, I am sorry to tell you this, but our attorneys have decided to go to court on Monday to file suit against you and Mr.

Haley for overdue rent. I am very sorry that we don't have any other choice."

That weekend, I went to church on Sunday, Shiloh Baptist, said a prayer of hope. That Sunday evening, I pondered why my good friend Alex Haley would leave me hanging in the lurch. Why? This left me disappointed and deeply concerned, as I went to bed about 11 p.m.

It was about an hour later that the phone rang. I wondered who could be calling at this late hour. I answered. The operator asked, in a foreign voice, "Is this Mr. Dukes?" I answered, "Yes, this is he." She said, "A Mr. Alex Haley is calling long distance from Trinidad." I then asked, "Is he calling collect?" The operator said, "No. I will put him on."

Alex said, "Brother Dukes, it is finished. *Roots* is finished!" And I said, "Alex, I can't believe this. It reminds me of what my grandma used to say, 'The Lord may not come when you want him but He is always on time.'"

Alex said, "Hey, my grandmother used to say the same."

On Monday, I went by the office of the manager of the Press Building and shared the relative good news. It was a matter of a few weeks that Alex did return.

During that year, 1976, Alex paid his back rent, and in 1977 he was the keynote speaker at a National

Press Club luncheon.[73] He told the audience that periodically, he would have to fly off to Africa to do more research or to some American city to deliver a lecture.

"The writing of the book took much, much longer that I'd anticipated, 12 years, "Haley explained. "I began giving lectures to keep myself afloat financially, but the lectures ate into my writing time." After the book was published and the television series captured the nation's attention, Haley was able to relax.

This was a moment of great triumph and the production of the history-making TV series of *Roots*. For the next two years, Alex remained a tenant in my office and I assisted in coordinating his busy public relations and his hectic speaking schedule. A major and thrilling highlight for me was being invited to join him and his two brothers, researcher and secretary on a triumphant return visit to the Village of Juffure in The Gambia, their ancestral home.[74]

On one occasion, he received an invitation from actress Elizabeth Taylor, who at the time lived in Washington as the wife of Senator John Warner. I joined Alex in visiting her at her Georgetown home.

---

[73] https://www.press.org/sites/default/files/speakers_fa.pdf

[74] This village is also spelled Juffureh.

She said she cried every night while watching the *Roots* TV series.

The TV series of *Roots* had tremendous impact on not only the African-American community but the entire world.

XVI.

Women Civil Rights Leaders

Tribute to Mrs. Coretta Scott King

I spent more than 20 years working very closely with Mrs. King, 10 years on her board at the Martin Luther King, Jr. Center for Non-violent Social Change and several years as a member of the King Holiday Commission. She was a magnificent lady of intellect, grace and class, dedicated to keeping the dream and legacy of her husband alive.

Mrs. King was most effective in lobbying for the passage of the King Holiday bill during the administration of President Ronald Reagan. She used her influence with Senate Majority Leader Robert "Bob" Dole to mobilize needed Republican support for the bill. She was relentless and much credit is due her, along with Congressman John Conyers, Jr., who introduced the bill in the House of Representatives and the national efforts of Stevie Wonder and so many others.

She was firmly committed to the cause of civil rights and worked hard in that regard. She shied away from publicity and was content to work in her own way as a highly-respected leader in both the Black and white communities. She was loyal to her husband in spite of the alleged defects of his human virtues.

At times, I was somewhat leery of a telephone call from Mrs. King because she had so much on her mind and would cover many related and some unrelated subjects. She was a good listener and accepted wise advice.

Mrs. King's Funeral a Farce—Same for Mrs. Rosa Parks

She was a most dignified lady and humble person, but her funeral was undignified and a travesty. And on the subject of funerals, Mrs. Rosa Parks' eight-hour funeral was a public farce, a disgrace, involving prominent people who did not know her. The entire episode was the worst kind of public relations coordinated by a close follower of hers from Los Angeles. What a shame! She, too, was a quiet, humble lady of dignity and grace.

Personal Friend and Advisor to Dr. Dorothy I. Height, National Council of Negro Women

Because Dr. Height considered me her personal public relations advisor, I enjoyed an exceptionally close relationship with her.[75] She would call early in the morning or late at night for advice. One of the last projects that I developed for her was an Obesity Prevention Project. She recalled losing 70 pounds at her doctor's advice for health reasons and decided to provide leadership in an effort to combat obesity among African Americans.

When her good live-in male friend, confidant, traveling mate died, Dr. Height called me early in the morning. She had a problem she wanted me to help resolve. The problem was in writing the obituary, how she could explain the relationship of a dear male friend living with her, who was always with her and on whom she depended for support. She was a single woman, the head of thousands of women members of the National Council of Negro Woman and the most prominent member and leader of Delta Sigma Theta Sorority, Inc.

---

[75] Dorothy Irene Height, an American administrator and educator, was a civil rights and women's rights activist specifically focused on the issues of African-American women. She was the president of the National Council of Negro Women for forty years.

Dr. Height was sensitive about how that should be explained in his obituary. After a discussion, we decided to describe him as a "longtime family friend." She was happy with that description.

Dr. Height, in her 90s, had the sharpest mind and in her dedication showed up at her office every day, fashionably attired in different color ensembles, always wearing a matching hat. A phenomenal woman of great history.

Personal Friend, Political Advisor, Co-worker, Dr. C. Delores Tucker, Co-Founder and President of the National Congress of Black Women, Chair, Democratic National Committee Black Caucus, Founder, Bethune DuBois Institute, NAACP leader

By far one of the most exciting relationships I had in Washington during a 25-year-period was with a phenomenal woman who did so much to advance the cause of African Americans. C. Delores worked full-time in the area of civil rights and political empowerment for Blacks.

As a political trailblazer, she was the first African-American woman in the nation to serve as Secretary of the Commonwealth of Pennsylvania and was the first Black vice chair of the Pennsylvania Democratic Party.[76]

C. Delores was a key member of the group of Black Democrats that organized the first National Conference of Black Democrats in Charlotte, North Carolina in the mid-1970s. This was the genesis of the DNC Black Caucus, of which she served as chair and a guiding leadership force or more than 10 years. As DNC Black Caucus Chair, she pushed hard for greater African American leadership and participation in the Democratic Party.

She was the catalyst, as president of the National Congress of Black Women, for bringing African-American women together for a power brunch during the Congressional Black Caucus Annual Legislative Conference. These women, elected officials from throughout the county, came, because of the leadership of C. Delores.

At one of her brunches, she honored the widows of Medgar Evers, Malcolm X, and Dr. King. The three widows, Myrlie Evers, Betty Shabazz, and Mrs. King had their daughters with them who spoke of those trying times. Daughters and mothers and most of the audience were in tears. That was one of those

---

[76] In 1971, Tucker became the first Black female Secretary of State under Pennsylvania Governor Milton Shapp.

special, unforgettable moments in our contemporary history.

She organized the Bethune-DuBois Institute for annual awards dinners to raise college scholarship funds for high school scholars.[77] When she passed, I was selected to serve as president of the organization.

One of her most important campaigns, in which her life was threatened, was against the obscene and misogynistic lyrics of Gangsta Rap.

She was a person of great compassion.

She did not wait until the death of Mrs. Rosa Parks to give honor to her and respond to Mrs. Parks' abject economic situation. On Sunday, February 4, 1990, C. Delores hosted a gala 77th birthday tribute to Mrs. Parks at the Kennedy Center and the funds went to Mrs. Parks.

One of C. Delores' last winning, but extended, battles before her death was getting the statute of Sojourner Truth in the U.S. Capitol.[78] It took C.

---

[77] Founded in 1986 by Dr. C. DeLores Tucker, the Bethune-DuBois Institute (BDI), a 501(c)(3) nonprofit organization, was established to sustain and magnify the legacies of two of America's greatest educators and leaders: Dr. Mary McLeod Bethune and Dr. W.E.B. DuBois. http://bethune-dubois.org/?page_id=4

[78] "Bust of Sojourner Truth Unveiled at U.S. Capitol," article in the *Washington Post* stated, "The idea began with the late C. DeLores Tucker, former chair of the National Congress of Black Women, a nonprofit advocacy organization devoted to advancing the causes of African-American women. Tucker originally wanted to add Truth's likeness to the eight-ton 'Portrait Monument' statues

Delores years to gain national and congressional support, especially among white and Black women in the U.S. Congress and a host of national organizations to support this effort.

C. Delores was a charming, elegantly dressed lady but could get into the political trenches and engaged in combat.

There were only a few days that C. Delores did not call, early in the morning or late at night, to run an idea by me. Her leadership legacy remains very deep with me. She was, indeed, a great American, a highly admired and respected human being, a devout Christian lady who was the daughter of a minister. This is my special tribute to her.

Marian Wright Edelman, President, Children's Defense Fund

I remember how Marian Wright, as head of a racially segregated Head Start program in Mississippi, would come to Vice President Humphrey's office for support. She would sit on the floor and plead her case.

---

of the heroines of the suffrage movement: Susan B. Anthony, Lucretia Mott and Elizabeth Cady Stanton."
http://www.washingtonpost.com/wp-dyn/content/article/2009/04/28/AR2009042803936.html

Mrs. Edelman has been remarkable for devoting her life and professional career to save our children. Over the past several decades, she has been effective in developing national public awareness and support for the millions of African-American children in critical need. She is one of the unsung heroes of the civil rights movement. And today she continues that fight "to save our endangered children."

XVII.

Challenging Public Relations Clients/Case Problems

Lever Brothers and a U.S. Senate Hearing on Detergents that Pollute

Lever Brothers, my second client, was concerned about US Senate Subcommittee hearings on detergents that allegedly pollute the environment. The hearing was headed by Senator Edmund Muskie, of Maine.

Having worked on the Capitol Hill, I knew, generally, that some senators had a tendency of taking home with them information or materials received at the end of the day. My young PR firm strategized with officials of Lever Brothers to have their new product neatly packaged and delivered to each 100 members of the U.S. Senate at about 5 p.m. Senator Muskie received his package and took it home and shared the product with his wife. She was impressed with the new Lever Brothers product and that had decisive impact on her husband and his hearings on the product. This became a part of my public relations learning process.

Educational Campaign to Introduce the New Child Development Associate Program.

In response to a national need for more trained professionals in early childhood education, OD&A was engaged by the U.S. Department of Education to develop a public education campaign to explain in detail the critical need for certified Child Development Associates. We had to overcome early opposition to the program by teacher unions and some institutions of higher learning. Again, this was part of my learning process about the human dynamics of public relations and strategic planning.

U.S. Senate Plan to Extend Broadcast Renewal from Three to Five Years

A U.S. Senate Subcommittee, chaired by Senator John Pastore (RI) began public hearings on a plan pushed by the broadcast industry to extend broadcast renewal from three to five years.

OD&A was engaged to develop and implement grassroots plans to aggressively fight the change in broadcast license renewal. This would be a Little David versus Goliath fight, my little firm against the powerful broadcast industry.

I recruited from Buffalo, New York a young man, an expert on broadcast issues and an excellent writer, to come to Washington to assist. He came with one piece of luggage and for a week or so camped out in my office.

We had a budget that allowed us to bring in witnesses to testify before the Subcommittee and prepared for them persuasive testimony. Since Senator Pastore, of New Jersey, was a very devout Catholic, I think the genius of our efforts was to bring to Washington to testify before his subcommittee nuns from New Jersey and Chicago. And they were tearful in raising moral issues and making broadcasters more insensitive and non-responsive to the needs of poor people. Their testimony carried the day, and the political move to extend broadcast license renewal from three to five years failed.[79] This, too, was part of my learning the basic fundaments of public relations.

The D.C. United Way Campaign versus the D.C. United Black Fund

In the early 1970's, as a consultant to the District of Columbia United Way, I was asked to

---

[79] The bill to extend broadcast stations' license terms to five years, from three years under the existing law, died at the end of the session. More info about this bill is available at https://library.cqpress.com/cqalmanac/document.php?id=cqal74-1222205

resolve a serious public confrontation with the D.C. Black United Fund, headed by Dr. Calvin Rolark, Publisher, *The Washington Informer* and president of the Black Fund. On Fridays, Dr. Rolark and D.C. Councilman Douglas Moore would hold downtown demonstrations in front of Riggs Bank, protesting the lack of support of the D.C. United Way for the Black community. On occasion, they would demonstrate in the bank.

The president of the United Way was Frank Wall, Jr., regional manager for IBM. He and Dr. Rolark had never met. I called my good friend Dr. Rolark and suggested an off-the-record meeting with Frank Wall. At first, Dr. Rolark was reluctant. He was not certain what it would accomplish. I suggested an early morning breakfast at a Black restaurant, Keys, on 7th near U Street, in the heart of Washington's Black community. I then approached Mr. Wall, who, too, had some anxiety about such a meeting. Finally, he was brave enough to accept. He then needed an outlined map to get from his downtown office on Connecticut Avenue to Keys restaurant, a place he had never heard of and a section of Washington he had never visited.

At 7 o'clock that morning, Mr. Wall was the first to arrive, and I was pleased to greet him at the restaurant. He had come by cab. Shortly thereafter, the vibrant Dr. Rolark arrived, went directly to Mr.

Wall, and said, "Frank, see, I am not a devil with horns." Probably for the first time in his life, Mr. Wall had a soul food breakfast of grits, eggs, sausage, and biscuits. He and Dr. Rolark had a friendly conversation and from that soul food breakfast meeting developed a partnership between the Black Fund and D.C. United Way. As I walked with Mr. Wall after the meeting to help him to safely catch a cab from D.C.'s Black ghetto, I once again whispered to myself, "Thank you, Jesus."

National Cancer Institute Joint Venture to Combat Cancer in the African American Community

In one of my most challenging and important public relations campaigns, my firm was engaged by the National Cancer Institute in 1985 to launch a campaign to educate African Americans that the "Big C," cancer, was preventable.[80] This campaign came as a result of a comprehensive study by then Secretary of Health and Human Services, Margaret M. Heckler, about the critical importance of information and education in preventive health practices.

---

[80] Research paper about this campaign can be found at: http://onlinelibrary.wiley.com/store/10.3322/canjclin.39.2.115/asset/1 15_ftp.pdf;jsessionid=E631329FE2DF71C7206C12336877260D.fo3t 01?v=1&t=j1y59fyi&s=a7c9620345c12a9b11935a8d4ea0010d20d78f8 d

In the African-American community, there was an existing fear about the "Big C" as a dreaded, terminal disease.

In response to the charge, I developed Joint Health Venture of 40 African-American organizations, for a grassroots education campaign emphasizing the importance of life style changes and preventive health as means of reducing the incidence of cancer. We involved the National Medical Association, the National Football Players Association, Aretha Franklin and Lena Horne, who both had lost sisters to cancer.

Noted Howard University cancer surgeon, Dr. LaSalle Leffall came to Detroit for a national kickoff of the campaign.

On a personal note, my mother had a reoccurrence of her breast cancer, and I told her of the campaign that cancer was curable. When she entered the hospital for her operation, she was up the next day talking to other patients with words of encouragement that cancer was not fatal but curable.

According to National Cancer Institute officials, the campaign helped change the attitudes of African Americans in dealing with what in the past was a dreaded disease that people did not want to discuss. A grassroots communications manual was developed as a result of the campaign.

The Washington Bullets of the National Basketball Association—Champion Celebration

When the Baltimore Bullets moved to Capital Centre in Largo, Maryland, a suburb of Washington, D.C., my firm was engaged by Washington Bullets owner and D.C. businessman Abe Pollin to represent the Bullets and introduced them to their new Washington, D.C. fans. I arranged a variety of activities, a goodwill tour of the Bullets in the city, a basketball game between Democratic and Republic members of Congress at Capital Center and any number of PR events.

However, my greatest challenge came in 1978 when the Bullets were battling Seattle for the NBA basketball championship. Entering the sixth championship game on Sunday at the Bullets' Capital Center, Seattle had a three to two game lead.

That Saturday night, I caught a red-eye flight from Las Vegas, where I was assisting Don King in a Sportsmanship Ball at Caesars Palace, in order to attend the mid-afternoon sixth game at Capital Center.

Thanks to the stellar play of Elvin Hayes, Wes Unseld, Phil Chenier, and Bobby Dandridge, the Bullets won the sixth game. And the fans chanted,

"The game isn't over until the Fat Lady sings."[81] And there was the "Fat Lady" symbolizing that in the audience in a special Middle Ages uniform.

After the exciting game, I went to owner Abe Pollin about possible plans for a victory celebration if the Bullets won the seventh game that Wednesday night in Seattle. Mr. Pollin waved me away, "Ofield, I am superstitious. I don't want to discuss that. Do what you need to do."

I then went to Bullets General Manager Bob Ferry and posed the same question. He, too, said he was superstitious about such matters and indicated, "Look, Ofield, we have great faith in your professionalism in representing us. Do what you need to do and just let us know."

That Monday, I went to my office at the National Press Building early and developed two plans: Plan A if they won—a victory celebration in Washington down Pennsylvania Avenue that Friday afternoon; And plan B, if they lost, having thousands of fans to greet the Bullets at Dulles Airport.

My next strategic step was to convene an urgent meeting on Tuesday morning at the D.C. City Hall,

---

[81] Coach Dick Motta of the Bullets explained during the postseason, following a loss to the Spurs, "The opera ain't over until the Fat Lady sings," which became a mantra for the Bullets. http://www.washingtontimes.com/news/2007/jun/4/20070604-125905-5648r/

co-hosted by Mayor Marion Barry, to discuss and get the input from representatives of city parade and police officials, representatives from Capitol Hill, the White House, and suburban jurisdictions.

The Tuesday meeting turned out to be a difficult challenge. There was some opposition to Plan A for a huge parade down Pennsylvania Avenue, with the Bullets leaving Capital Centre in Largo, Maryland at 3 p.m. that Friday afternoon, and arriving in the District at about 3:30 p.m., down Pennsylvania Avenue, arriving at the District Building for a mass 4 p.m. rally. The first challenge came from representatives of the U.S. Senate and the House of Representatives, insisting that the first stop should be the U.S. Capitol for a rally hosted by members of Congress. The Mayor's people were vehement in their opposition to that. So, I interrupted the debate to say, forcefully, the first stop would be City Hall.

White House representatives said President Jimmy Carter had a tight schedule, and if we were to visit the White House it had to be before 5 p.m. They suggested a White House visit prior to a rally at City Hall. I held to my decision of a 4 p.m. rally at City Hall.

Then the D.C. Police Chief rose and said he had a serious problem with a parade down Pennsylvania and rally at City Hall during a Friday rush hour. He said this would be a great imposition on his police force, would tie up traffic for hours, and he was against it. I indicated that we could not move a victory celebration to Saturday, because the NBA owners would be meeting in Hawaii on Saturday and the players would be returning to their respective homes.

The police chief was adamant. There was a long pause. I then stood up and thought for a moment, and then went to the chief and said. "Chief, I think you're right about this possibly being a difficult imposition on your police force. But Chief, I remember when tens of thousands of college students invaded the city to demonstrate against the Vietnam War. Chief, I also remember how hundreds of truckers came to the city, and your police officers were great in handling such disruptions. And I think you said then that your police department was number one in the nation."

The police chief looked at me, and said, "You're right, Mr. Dukes, we have a great police department in the District, and I am certain we can handle a victory parade for the Bullets at the time you suggest." Whew! I said to myself.

Prior to the Wednesday's night game in Seattle, I called Bob Zurfluh, the Bullets' PR director, and explained to him Plans A & B.

In the 7th game, Wes Unseld was a star in
helping the Bullets to win the 1978 NBA
championship.

That Friday, more than 100,000 Bullets fans
lined up on Pennsylvania Avenue, peered out of
windows of federal buildings, to watch the parade.
And at City Hall (District Building), there were
15,000 people, and the largest crowd to gather there
since the end of World War II. At the next stop,
President Carter greeted owner Abe Pollin, the
Bullets, and the Fat Lady in the East Room where
you had more than 200 White House staff cheering
the home team.

The third stop was Capitol Hill, where members
of Congress greeted the Bullets and the final top was
a rally at Robert F. Kennedy Stadium, where the only
incident was for Elvin Hayes to leave the stage to
greet fans and dislocating the barricade.

The entire victory celebration was televised live
and everything went off on schedule. And I was one
happy trooper.

Don King, the highly successful boxing promoter with the FBI on his trail

One day in 1977, I received a surprise visitor at my office. It was none other than the incomparable and highly successful boxing promoter, Don King.

Mr. King explained that he was in the neighborhood and just wanted to say "hello" but he did mention "a little problem." The FBI was hot on his trail, "harassing the shit out of me with all kinds of criminal allegations." He needed some help in "cleaning up his image."

I told him I would be delighted to assist. He said, simply, "That's a deal," shook my hand walked out of my office. At the end of the day, as I was cleaning my desk to leave, I noticed a strange white enveloped on the edge of my desk. I picked up the envelop, opened it, and to my surprise, it contained in crisp American currency $15,000.00. This obviously was left by Mr. King.

Mr. King's controversial background includes a prison term for murder and a reputation of being a hustler. So, my first challenge was to somehow change his public image. He was a bright, articulate, charming man, colorful, super dynamic. One of my first assignments was to get him to speak before an assembly of students at Howard University.

A physical characteristic of Don King was his bushy hair protruding from his head. About 2,000 curious students at Howard crowded Cramton Auditorium to check out this flamboyant boxing promoter. Mr. King began by saying to the students that what's on your head doesn't count. It's what in your head that counts. Then he went on to quote a half-dozen Greek philosophers, talked about his dealings with the Rockefeller brothers in New York and his Christian values of treating others as he would want to be treated.

The Howard University newspaper, *The Hilltop*, wrote that King told the students how he made four years of incarceration for second degree murder manslaughter work in his favor by reading read Voltaire, Chaucer, Gibran, King, Kennedy, Dante, and all those cats. When he came out, he was armed with an atom bomb of knowledge.

And then, in his generosity, he pulled out a bunch of checks, and announced from the stage $250,000 in contributions to various Black institutions, including the Howard University Hospital, the Howard University School of Communications, the Martin Luther King, Jr. Center for Nonviolent Social Change, among others. He was most persuasive and received a standing ovation from the students.

I arranged for him to be a guest at the annual convention of the Black press, the National Newspapers Publishers Association, and he surprised them with a $50,000 contribution.

On one occasion Rev. Jesse Jackson called me about needing funds for the burning the mortgage of his National Rainbow Coalition in Chicago. I called Mr. King, who agreed to visit the mortgage burning ceremony. He not only made a $50,000 contribution but brought five of his fighters who each make financial contributions. We changed Mr. King's image to a generous, kind-hearted philanthropist, a scholarly man with a penchant for Black history. I also had Mr. King depositing funds in Black banks.

Due to my own political contacts at the Democratic National Committee, I arranged for Mr. King to join the DNC Finance Committee at a level of $15,000 that allowed him to receive an invitation from President Jimmy Carter for dinner at the White House.

According to my files, on October 4, 1978, Mr. King, at a White House reception, gave Mrs. Carter a letter for the President, asking him to support a special tribute to Joe Louis in November, hosted by Frank Sinatra and Muhammad Ali, at Caesars Palace in Las Vegas, which was the main locale for Mr. King's championship fights.

My files on Don King also indicate that I arranged for him to testify before the House Committee on Education and Labor Committee on Labor Standards on a proposed Federal Boxing Control Act of 1979 and an eventual meeting with the chairman of that Committee, Rep. Edward P. Beard. That bill was not passed.[82]

King made boxing history by introduction one million dollar salaries for championship bouts that elevated him to the country's most successful boxing promoter.

From these various activities, Mr. King developed a solid reservoir of goodwill in the Black community as an "outstanding American citizen." The FBI continued to investigate the activities of Mr. King but he was never convicted or jailed for illegal behavior.

When my friend Cathy Hughes, as a radio manager, needed additional funds to purchase her first radio station, WOL, I called Mr. King and he promptly sent a cashier's check for $1,000. Ms. Hughes financial advisors refused to accept Mr. King's check, suggesting that it was not clean. Mr. King and I were both disappointed by this.

---

[82] More info about this bill is available at:
https://www.congress.gov/bill/96th-congress/house-bill/2726

I have been pushing him hard to do a book on his remarkable life and career, without any success to date.

Republic of Liberia—Improving Its International Image

In 1979, the Minister of Foreign Affairs for the Republic of Liberia visited my office to discuss his county's race riots and other problems and the interest of his president, William Tolbert, to hire an American minority firm to improve Liberia's public image.

I developed a comprehensive proposal that went to President Tolbert. Based on the proposal, I was invited to Monrovia, Liberia to meet with him. He signed the contract and for the next two years my firm provided a wide range of public relations services for Liberia.

This included a red-carpet visit to the City of Detroit, where President Tolbert received an honorary degree from Wayne State University and met with the Overseas Investment Group at General Motors. We assisted in developing greater awareness of the historical association of Liberia and America and an evolving constituency for Liberia in this country.

Then the ugliest kind of tragedy happened to
the country. Sgt. Doe assassinated top officials of the
Liberian government and other leaders. On this day
of infamy and great tragedy for the people of Liberia,
I resigned from my contract. Having any association
with the Sgt. Doe regime was unthinkable and
directly contrary to my sense of personal and
business integrity.

Montel Williams, TV Host—Improving His National Image

In 1994, I received a call from a vice president
of Viacom to engage my firm to help improve the
national image of syndicated TV host Montel
Williams. The objective was to increase TV show
viewership of his daily show.

I arranged for Montel to come to Washington,
D.C., a major TV market, for a series of media
interviews and public appearances. Since I was
teaching public relations at The American
University, I invited him to speak to students there
and also at Howard University.

However, on the Howard campus, female
students had strong feelings about Black men
crossing over to date and marry women of another
race. These students were aware of the fact that
Montel, a Black man from Baltimore, had married a

white hoochie-coochie dancer from Las Vegas and eagerly awaited his arrival on campus

In the limousine on our way to Howard University, I advised Montel of the strong sentiment of female students, in particular. As we arrived, we were surrounded by dozens of students waiting outside for our arrival. Inside, the room was crowded with predominantly female students who seemed organized to jump him on the marriage issue.

Montel was cool. In his remarks, he told of a difficult period in his life and career, when he was down, depressed, lonely, and not certain of what to do in his life. He then asked if any students ever felt that way. He explained that a person, a stranger, a woman befriended him. She offered her unselfish friendship; she offered emotional support, gave him a sense of confidence, and then, he said, she gave him her pure, genuine love. Montel said for a man down that her friendship and love meant so much—to have a sincere, honest commitment of love.

Then he asked the audience if they ever had such a love commitment or relationship with honesty and integrity with fellows on campus. And there was a chorus of "No!"

Montel went on to say that God-given love transcends race, has no barriers, and can be a special and sacred thing. After his remarks on love, he was mobbed by the female students; some asked questions and others wanted his autograph.

Montel left Howard with a sigh of relief. We both agreed that having honesty and integrity in life were more than PR virtues.

Providing Entertainment for More Than 100 U.S. Department of Labor Job Corps Centers

With a contract with the U.S. Department of Labor, OD&A recruited and arranged top entertainment for more than 100 Job Corps Centers throughout the United States. This entailed strict management and the coordination of logistics in travel, housing, feeding, and maintaining a strict tour schedule for the different groups of entertainers.

Our concern was the providing the type of entertainment enjoyed by a diversity of Job Corps members. And that was a challenge.

Communication Strategy for The National Capital Monumental Core Plan—A Major Event in American History

In 1994, the U.S. National Capital Planning Commission had the congressional responsibility of planning a new plan for Washington's monuments, the mall and the federal city. It was under the

guidance of Presidents George Washington and
Thomas Jefferson that Pierre L'Enfant developed in
1791 the original plan for the Washington, D.C. as
the nation's capital.[83] In 1901, President Theodore
Roosevelt supported and the U.S. Senate
commissioned the McMillan Plan which expanded
the L'Enfant plan to include the present National
Mall.[84]

The historic task of the U.S. National Capital
Planning Commission to craft a third plan for the
federal city was a daunting one for commission
members. In that connection, my firm was hired to
develop a comprehensive communication strategy to
inform the Congress, White House, the Federal
City, D.C. officials and residents and the national
public of the development of new Monumental Core
Plan.

This required attending numerous meetings of
the National Capital Planning Commission (NCPC),
developing an initial internal communication
strategy, a comprehensive external communication
plan for methodical implementation, and a media
strategy. This included NCPC briefings and media
training, message development, identification of "red

---

[83] https://founders.archives.gov/documents/Washington/05-09-02-
0124

[84] http://urbanplanning.library.cornell.edu/DOCS/parkcomm.htm

flag" issues, production of appropriative materials, series of public briefings in each of the city's eight wards, political briefings, public regional hearings, media briefings, with the support of the NCPC staff.

This was a two-year project that really tested my public relations skills. And our communication plan was successfully implemented and the new National Monument Core Plan enthusiastically accepted by the public.

Grassroots National Public Education Campaign on Redesigned American Currency in Partnership with Burson-Marsteller and the U.S. Department of the Treasury to Prevent Worldwide Counterfeiting

With an alarming increase in the counterfeiting of American currency in this country and throughout the world, the U.S. Department of the Treasury decided to launch a grassroots public information and education campaign to introduce redesigned American currency to combat counterfeiting. Burson-Marsteller was hired as the lead public relations agency and my firm was invited by Burson-Marsteller to join in partnership. Beginning with the redesign of the $100 bill, my firm participated with Burson-Marsteller in subsequent campaigns to introduce redesigned $50, $20, $10 and $5 notes over a 10-year period.

This grassroots communications campaign entailed the highest level of strategic creativity, innovative public relations tactics and techniques, effective management, strict financial accounting, and maximum measurable results. This was public relations at its highest level, which was a challenge I gladly accepted.

An African-American Buckle-Up Campaign for the National Highway Traffic Safety Administration, of the US Department of Transpiration

In 1999, one of the significant diversity efforts was the launching of a nationwide campaign directed at the African American community to improve seat belt use by African Americans that could save as many as 1,200 lives per year and prevent 26,000 injuries at a cost savings of nearly $2.6 billion.

Joining Transportation Secretary Rodney Slater and National Highway Traffic Safety Administration (NHTSA) Administrator Richard Martinez at a July press conference were U.S. Surgeon General Dr. David Satcher, General Motors Vice President Roderick Gillum, Meharry Medical College President Dr. John Maupin, and Congressional Black Caucus member U.S. Rep. Eddie Bernice Johnson.

My firm had the responsibility of developing a year-long communications strategy to encourage

African Americans to buckle up. We learned the importance of creativity and credibility. The main advocates of our strategy were two of the most popular and credible African Americans in the news at that time, tennis pros Venus and Serena Williams. They were featured in posters and radio spots that proved most effective. We also did a special taping of the father of a son who was tragically killed in a car accident when he failed to use a seat belt.

Theatrical Press Agent—A New Public Relations Challenge

In 1974, I was contacted by Moe Septee, who was producing a musical production in Philadelphia, called "Bubbling Brown Sugar." Somehow, Mr. Septee got my name from someone because he was planning to bring the show to Washington, D.C. and needed public relations support.

In his telephone call to me, Mr. Septee asked if I was in a union. I said no but I would explore that. I was not aware of the union requirements of a press agent. I called my ex-boss, Senator Hubert H. Humphrey, who gave me a contact with the National Association of Theatrical and Press Agents in New York. Added Humphrey, "Tell him I asked you to call."

I made the call, spoke with the executive
director of the union, and was told that in order to
join the union I needed to be invited by two union
members to do a three-year internship. I mentioned
to him that Mr. Humphrey asked me to call and that
I had worked for Mr. Humphrey when he was Vice
President. The executive director of the union
responded, "Hey, Hubert Humphrey is my man. I am
going to send you some forms to fill out, get them
back to me, and I will get you a union card right
away." In life, sometimes it's not what you know but
who you know that makes a difference.

I later learned that there were only two African
Americans belonging to the union and the executive
director of a main Black theatrical organization in
Harlem was doing his internship.

Within two weeks, I received my union card
and then went to Philadelphia and met with Mr.
Septee. I agreed to be the theatrical public relations
agent for "Bubbling Brown Sugar" in its engagement
at the National Theatre in Washington.

This was something entirely new for me. But I
prided myself in being a quick learner. I developed a
strategy for promoting the musical in all segments of
Washington. A main focus was to "paper the crowd"
in the pre-opening rehearsals with an emphasis on
word of mouth.

We planned a grand, red carpet opening, with guests including members of Congress, D.C. elected officials, business and community leaders, heads of social and civic organizations and pastors. Prior to the opening, a good friend, "Petey" Greene, a highly popular grassroots activist and radio and TV host and a member of the "sporting crowd," called and asked if I would provide him complimentary tickets to invite a few of his friends. I asked how many tickets? He said about a dozen.

At the grand opening of "Bubbling Brown Sugar" at the National Theatre that evening came a cavalcade of people from all sectors of Washington society, the high and influential, common folks, and a strange group. Arriving in chartreuse Cadillacs and dressed in flashy attire were "Petey" Greene's guests, pimps and prostitutes. They were all welcomed.

The show was fantastic. The cast was multi-talented.

Early the next morning, a Sunday morning, "Petey" Greene called from some all-night spot. He said his guests were still beaming about "Bubbling Brown Sugar." He said they would spread the word about how great the show was.

The word did spread and for the next six weeks, "Bubbling Brown Sugar" was a sellout. After it left Washington, it became a hit on Broadway. I learned that word of mouth, with positive media reviews, make a big difference in theatrical public relations. I did spend the next year handling a number of plays at the National Theatre and working closely with Woodie King, Jr. and his National Black Touring Circuit. King is a noted pioneering show producer in New York City.

Black Public Relations Society of Washington, D.C.—Expanding Black Opportunities in Field of Public Relations

One of the Black pioneers in public relations from Los Angeles, Pat Tobin, CEO, Pat Tobin & Associates, and the founder of the National Black Public Relations Society, began pushing me in the early 1990s to organize a chapter of Black public relations practitioners in Washington. She would come to Washington for the Congressional Black Caucus Annual Legislative Conference, representing her client, Toyota. We would meet, on one occasion with the executive director of the Public Relations Society of America.

Finally, I agreed. And in October, 1992, I convened a meeting of Blacks in public relations. And to my amazement, we had a standing room only crowd, at a downtown hotel ballroom, of more than 200. They were all excited about organizing and moving into the mainstream of public relations practice. Our meeting became so important the *Washington Post* did two articles on our efforts. A major story in the business section of the *Washington Post* read: "Breaking the color Barrier in PR—Minority Firms Mobilize to Expand Their Role in D.C." Another Post article in February, 1993, headlined: "Black PR Firms Charge Business Bias." A major trade association publication headlined: "D.C. Blacks Form a Public Relations League of Their Own—Blacks 'Invisible' in D.C. PRSA, say founder Ofield Dukes."

We ended up developing a strong, cohesive chapter of the Black Public Relations Society in Washington, which became the largest such chapter in the country. Our activities included workshops on business development and marketing, involvement of major public relations firms on diversity and minority and intern recruitment. We had a membership of more than 300 and regular monthly meetings, with high-powered guest speakers. We were quite successful in gaining national attention about the barriers facing Blacks in the public relations industry and working with local PR firms in the recruitment of minority interns and professionals.

XVIII.

Death of Senator Hubert H. Humphrey—Presenting his Final Two Speeches

Sadly, Senator Humphrey was diagnosed as having cancer in 1977. In spite of his illness, I had been involved in arranging for the Senator to speak at the mid-winter meeting of the National Newspaper Publishers Association (NNPA) in Miami. NNPA represented the trade association of Black editors and publishers, very close friends and supporters of Senator Humphrey. This was a Friday night. On Saturday, Mrs. Coretta Scott King and a host of Black leaders planned to honor him at a special leadership meeting at Ebenezer Baptist Church in Atlanta.

That week, Senator Humphrey was in a hospital in Minneapolis. During the week, I spoke with the senator's office every day regarding his condition and his planned speeches before NNPA and the Black leadership meeting in Atlanta.

It was decided in mid-week that his sister, Frances Howard, would represent him at both events. However, that Friday morning word came that the Senator's condition had worsened and his sister, Frances, called me to say that she was flying to Minneapolis to be at her brother's bedside. She told me that I would have to give both speeches on his behalf.

There was a touch of divine irony that Friday night, January 13, 1978. At the exact moment Senator Humphrey died, he was being honored by some of his most loyal friends and supporters, hundreds of Black editors and publishers who during his vice presidency were invited once or twice a year to Washington to meet with him and President Johnson.

I had the sad but special honor of giving Senator Humphrey's last two speeches before Blacks who deeply appreciated his unflinching commitment and courageous support of civil rights during his distinguished public service career.

The meeting of Black leaders at Ebenezer Church became the first memorial service in honor of Mr. Humphrey. Black editors and publishers and leaders at Ebenezer Church remembered how Humphrey, as the brash but courageous Mayor of Minneapolis, at the 1948 Democratic National Convention led a bitter fight for a minority plank on civil rights that led to South Carolina Senator Strom Thurman walking out of the convention. This 1948

convention was one of the finest moments of
Humphrey's political career when he took the
podium in a steaming hot convention hall in
Philadelphia and made his famous remarks that it's
time for the Democratic Party to move out of the
shadows of States' rights and into the bright sunshine
of civil rights.[85]

Democratic Party officials had many anxieties
about Humphrey's bold move in light of an expected
tough election between President Harry S. Truman
and Republican presidential candidate Thomas
Dewey. The strong feeling was without the support
of southern states President Truman would not stand
a chance of being re-elected. The early prediction
was Dewey would win. Truman's come-from-behind
victory shocked the political world and the country.

Having the opportunity of working for Vice
President Humphrey and becoming closely
acquainted with him and his sincere commitment to
public service and civil rights was indeed a
remarkable experience for the young man from
racially segregated Crenshaw County in rural
Alabama and Detroit's ghetto.

---

[85] Full speech is available online at
https://www.youtube.com/watch?v=8nwIdIUVFm4

XIX.

Beginning of Family Life in Washington D.C.

Life as a Bachelor in Washington, D.C.

Although I was featured in *Ebony* magazine and *Washingtonian* magazine as a single, eligible bachelor, that never became an important part of my life style or social focus.[86] I had a variety of female friends in the context of friendship defined by one of my favorite philosophers, Kahlil Gibran—be sincere and honest in giving the best of you to your friends. And I was motivated to treat all my female friends like I wanted someone to treat my sister or my daughter.

Also, I must add that I was inclined to maintain a sense of independence—no romantic commitments. I was part of a Sunday afternoon tennis group of mainly female friends, and I was often called by female acquaintances about job opportunities and advice and emotional support for

---

[86] He was featured in *Washingtonian* magazine in 1974 and in *Ebony Magazine* multiple times. His obituary in *The Washington Post* on December 9, 2011 by Matt Schudel included mention of *Ebony*'s rating him as one of Washington's most popular bachelors.

the challenges they were facing. I should also add that I did have the habit of mailing at least 70 Saint Valentine's Day cards and Mother's Day cards in a platonic way to female friends, plus hundreds of Christmas and New Year's cards to a list of friends. On one occasion, I received a call from a mother of two sons who, tearfully, said my Mother's Day card was the only one she received, and she was touched by it.

In time, my bachelorhood came to an unplanned but happy end.

Courtship and Marriage

In the pursuit of Kahlil Gibran's dissertation on friendship in his popular book, *The Prophet*, I met an intellectually, captivating, gracious and charming lady who came to Washington from Detroit as a Health & Education & Welfare Fellow, with a Ph.D. degree from the University of Michigan. She was Dr. Rosa Lee Clausell, a native of Wilmington, North Carolina.[87] She was from a family of twelve and the first to attend and graduate from college, Madonna Catholic College in Detroit's suburbs. She became a friend not to be denied.

---

[87] Rosa was divorced before marrying Ofield and hyphenated her last name as Trapp-Dukes.

After a wonderful friendship and socially dating for about two years, Rosa posed a direct and challenging question: Did I have any plans for the eventual direction of the friendship? Was I ever interested in marriage and parenthood? And there I was in 1974, in my early 40s in cruise control in life.

That December, I pondered an ideal Christmas gift for Rosa, with the questions she posed running recklessly across an uncertain mind. So, in shopping for a gift, I entered a jewelry store in downtown Washington, and looked at some rings, but I was not certain about making a purchase.

However, the next Saturday, with a little bit more courage, and assurance, I returned to the jeweler, with her ring size, and purchased a ring, a sapphire. Since I was going to Detroit to be with my family for Christmas, I had the sapphire ring wrapped in a number of boxes and left it with Rosa to be opened on Christmas day.

That Christmas day when I called Rosa from Detroit, she was very cool and questioned the exact purpose of the ring. I stumbled badly in responding to her question. I think my answer was the ring, a sapphire, was part of the diamond family. Rosa said, pointedly, that she would not wear the ring until I was clear of its purpose and had a chance to discuss its meaning. That discussion was in February when I agreed that we were officially engaged to be married.

The marriage took palace in Detroit in August of 1975 at New Calvary Baptist Church, attended by about 1,000.[88] A luxurious reception was held in a mansion overlooking the Detroit River. We had purchased a home in an exclusive section of Falls Church, Virginia, the Lake Barcroft area, where only two other Blacks lived, Supreme Court Justice Thurgood Marshall and ABC local TV anchor Paul Barry. We had a real estate agent friend to say only that the interested purchaser of a house in Lake Barcroft had been a member of the staff of Vice President Humphrey. There was no racial identity. So, when Rosa and I attended our first meeting of the Lake Barcroft Association, some were surprised, but we were warmly greeted. The number of Blacks in the area never increased beyond the three as long as we lived there.

In celebration of our marriage, a Washington reception was held at the National Press Club, attended by a VIP crowd of the mayor, city council members, Vice President Humphrey, representatives of my clients—the General Manager and players from the Washington Bullets and the cast of the Broadway-bound play, "Bubbling Brown Sugar."

---

[88] The Trapp-Dukes relationship and marriage was captured in the January 1983 *Ebony* article, "First Marriage After 40," by Lynn Norment, p. 29.

Fatherhood—Birth of Daughter, Roxi

In 1983, our daughter, Roxi, was born. And this was the beginning of the most exciting part of my life, parenthood. Rosa spent considerable time selecting a nanny for Roxi, finally agreeing on a wonderful lady, Nellie Valez, from Columbia, South America.

In Roxi's infancy, I had the night shift, from midnight to 6 a.m. So, I learned the fine art of changing diapers and tending to her after-hours needs. Nellie was on duty from 8 a.m. to 6 p.m. I made it a top priority to leave my office to be home by 6 p.m. to take care of Roxi, until her mother arrived from her night classes as a professor at Howard University.

I strongly felt that I needed to be as successful as a parent as I was as a business person and that family responsibility was of uppermost importance. The birth of Roxi and our evolving relationship was the first in a series of mountaintop experiences.

XX.

A Period of Dark Despair— The *Washington North Star* Newspaper—Collapse of Marriage

Nine years into the marriage, some difference developed. In the marriage, I learned you need to remain focused, to work hard to repair any cracks, any languishing problems. Rosa was having her challenges at Howard University, and I had assumed what turned out to be an impossible challenge at my office, a decision to start a newspaper, the *Washington North Star* newspaper.

As a former journalist, I had a burning passion to move back into the field of journalism. I had spent time meeting with a group of colleagues as potential investors in the newspaper venture. When they were slow to respond, I made a decision to proceed. I proceeded to hire a staff of professional reporters from the defunct *Washington Star*.

The first edition of the *North Star*, named after the anti-slavery newspaper of abolitionist Frederick

Douglass, was a 48-page tabloid and a smash. Articles appeared about the new *North Star* in the *Washington Post*.[89] *Washington Post* Publisher Donald Graham sent a handwritten note of congratulations. There were radio and television interviews and countless invitation to speak at meetings and awards presentations.

I struggled financially to publish the *North Star* for six months without any outside support, losing more than $100,000. I made serious mistakes of paying the printer instead of the mortgage company. My PR business suffered. I fell behind in my Press Building rent. My office furniture was repossessed as I was forced to move my office to our home. My luxury car, a Cadillac, was repossessed and because of being months behind in the mortgage payments, the home was about to be foreclosed.

At home, creditors kept calling and during that period of midnight darkness, of distraught and disillusionment, my four-year-old daughter, Roxi, would open the bedroom door where I was trying to find my way. She would simply say, "Daddy, I love you," and then close the door behind her. This was

---

[89] Robinson, Eugene. "The North Star." *Washington Post*, November 25, 1981. Accessed May 27, 2017.
https://www.washingtonpost.com/archive/local/1981/11/25/the-north-star/0e3a0124-ff9a-4362-b3bd-52cef330b29a/?utm_term=.f96085e6e16d.

my source of inspiration. She remained a part of my mountaintop experience even when I was at such a low point.

Even during those worst of times, I did not lose faith in my God and faith in my ability to find my way from the lonely, dark, dreary shadows of the valley, back to the mountaintop of my profession. I was down but not out and thought of the poetic words of "Invictus"—"It matters not how straight the gate, how charred with punishment the scroll; I am the master of my fate, I am the captain of my soul."

Rosa and I had a civil discussion about our marriage, without any rancor, and decided to separate.

Rosa, Roxi and Nellie, our nanny, moved to a home in the District. I was able to rent a one-room bedroom in Alexandria, Virginia until I could afford to move into a condo in southwest Washington.

In the meantime, Rosa and I maintained a very cordial and civil friendship in the separation. I assumed responsibility for picking up Roxi every day from the Foggy Bottom preschool. Rosa would come by after her class at Howard University to join us for dinner and to take Roxi home with her.

When Roxi entered middle school at Holy Trinity School in Georgetown, because Rosa lived in suburban Fort Washington, Maryland and faced heavy traffic incoming to the District, a joint decision was made for Roxi to live with me. That continued when Roxi entered St. John's College High School. It was during that period that I learned how to be a caring, sharing father, who never used a babysitter but took my daughter with me to business meetings and social gatherings.

Parental Challenges

There were parental challenges. As a student at Holy Trinity, the Catholic parish of the Kennedy family, Roxi was elected president of the school's student council. However, the school principal, for some strange reason, decided to annul the election. That not only upset Roxi but prompted us to have an urgent meeting with the principal. We were angry parents but maintained our anger in a civil, diplomatic way. We wanted to know why she wanted to change the results of the election. Was it because Roxi had become the first African American to be elected president of Holy Trinity's student council?

Rosa and I suggested to the principal that we did not want the situation to become public to tarnish the reputation of the school. We also expressed our concern about some of the white students calling Roxi "a nerd" based on her high academic performance. The principal could not explain any rational reason for changing the results of the election, and Roxi remained president of the student council.

While at the school, Rosa and I met with one of Roxi's teachers, a priest, and we inquired about the conduct of female students toward Roxi, calling her a nerd. The priest had an interesting response. "Please don't be offended. Some pre-teenage girls are little bitches, going through all kinds of changes. Things work out OK eventually."

On another occasion, Roxi, as president of Holy Trinity's student council and, was being harassed by several boys. She came home in tears. I reminded her that her grandmother got up every morning with her God-given joy and would not allow anyone to mess or tamper with it.

When Roxi returned to school and in presiding at a Council meeting was met with similar harassment. She told me she went to the boys and told them, "Don't f___ with my God-given joy."

In shock, I told my dear daughter, that her grandmother Dukes and Jesus did not use that type of language.

Roxi responded, "Daddy, you sometimes have to use street language to get your point across."

She hugged me, and we both laughed.

Growth and Blossoming of Daughter, Roxi

From her birth, every New Year's I developed and mailed to friends a colorful update on Roxi's growth and development. Many people say they maintained a collection of Roxi's New Year's cards, always carrying photos and updates.

In 1990, *USA Today* did a special feature on Rosa, Roxi and me, with a photo, under a title "Children bind parents to lifetime relationship."[90] The article read, in part, "Divorced parents with kids still have a relationship 'until death do us part.' Ofield Dukes and his former wife, Rosa Trapp-Dail, continue to co-parent the daughter, Roxi, 9."

I was quoted as saying, "It is tremendously important to Roxi that she understands and feels the spirit of cooperation and the friendship between her mom and dad. That contributes to Roxi's peace of mind." Added Rosa, "We all have a good relationship. Both parents agree to live lives that make sense."

After two years of legal separation, at the divorce hearing, the judge raised a question about joint custody of Roxi. He said he did not think that would work. Rosa rose from her seat and said,

---

[90] Ribbon, Lable. "Life After Divorce." *USA Today*, October 8, 1990, p. 2D.

"Judge, Mr. Dukes is as good a parent as I am." The judge promptly said, "Divorce granted."

Roxi, as young multi-talented performer, auditioned to do her senior high year at the North Carolina School of the Arts and was accepted in the drama department. She entered Howard University as the most talented freshman in singing, acting and dancing.

One summer she studied Shakespeare at the University of Oxford in England and another summer she was studying ballet at the International School of Ballet in Paris. In her senior year at Howard, Roxi performed in a number of dramatic plays. She was named the best actress in the senior class.

After graduation, Roxi performed in New York City and received rave reviews for her performance at a mean-spirited, brutal and philosophical dope peddler in "Breast Boom" at the Studio Theatre in Washington, D.C. She played leading roles at the Folger Shakespeare Theatre performing in "Much Ado About Nothing" and "A Midsummer Night's Dream" and was Assistant Director of "King Lear."

While working in my office, she met Michael Victorian who was doing an internship in my office as a Howard University public relations scholar and major. They developed a social relationship over time.

He called for a meeting with me to discuss the evolving relationship. He said, "Mr. Dukes, you have told your daughter, Roxi not to waste her time with fellows without integrity, intelligence and respect for her. Mr. Dukes, I have integrity, I think I am intelligent, and I have a lot of respect for your daughter." A year or so later, Roxi and Michael were married. In May of 2007, they became parents of Michael Dukes Victorian. They now live in Baton Rouge, Louisiana, his hometown, where he is in law school, and Roxi teaches dance and drama and continues her performing arts career.[91]

---

[91] In 2011, they lived in Baton Rouge. Michael completed his JD in 2014 and has practiced law since.

XXI.

Emerging from the Depth of Darkness to a Bright Light of Restoration

I remember from my youth an adage of Confucius—The glory is not in never falling, but the glory is getting up every time you fall.

Getting up and finding your way back is an awesome challenge...awesome. There are so many factors involved. The first of which is determination.

After my period of gloom and darkness. I had intense determination, a burning sensation to get back on a more positive track. In following my basic principles, I got up every day with a passion for excellence, to work hard, to maintain the highest professional standards, not to compromise my sense of integrity under any circumstances, to practice the strictest time management and organization, and to strive to be one step strategically ahead of my clients and in providing services to them. Most important was interpersonal relations, always maintaining a calm disposition, learning the art of listening, maintaining effective mutual communications, and having a positive attitude and approach.

This goes back to having a compelling faith in my ability to deal with life's adversities. I continue to embrace what I call the three C's—Confidence, Competence, and the ability to be Competitive.

I worked diligently to make the next 20 years of my period of restoration to be lucrative times for Ofield Dukes & Associates. My clients included: Sony Music Entertainment, the Washington Bullets, a 10-year partnership with the U.S. Department of Treasury and Burson-Marsteller, Pfizer, the Pharmaceutical Manufacturers Association, Pasteur Merieux Connaught, R.J. Reynolds, the Congressional Black Caucus and Foundation (editing the newsletter), Howard University, Montel Williams/Viacom, Time Warner, Prince, Rev. Leon Sullivan and his International Foundation for Education and Self-Help, the National Cancer Institute, the National Capital Planning, and Aretha Franklin.

During this 20-year period in the early 1990s, I began teaching public relations as an adjunct professor at The American University. My activities as a communications consultant with the Democratic Party increased after the 1988 meeting convened by C. Delores Tucker in Atlanta. There was the 1988 exciting trip as a part of Mrs. King's entourage to

South Africa before the end of apartheid. Also, in 1988, I coordinated the public relations for the 25th anniversary of the Great March on Washington.

In 1988, I had the pleasure, as a member of the Congressional Black Caucus Board of Directors, in planning and coordinating the 80th birthday salute to U.S. Supreme Court Justice Marshall, which was an extraordinary event because this was one of the very few times he has agreed to such a public event.

In 1994, Pedro Alfonso, President and CEO of Dynamic Concepts, in the District and I became the first Black business executives to be selected by the Japan-United States Business Council for a 10-day trip to Japan to learn how to do business with Japanese companies. We were part of a group of 25 American business executives on the VIP, all-expenses-paid trip.

Professional Relationship with Howard University

In 2001, I was invited by the Dr. Jannette L. Dates, dean of the Howard University School of Communications, to serve as co-chairman of the 30th anniversary of the School. I had 40 of my former PR students to commit to a contribution of $1,000.00 each to the School.

After the death of my good friend, Grace Halsell, former White House aide to President

Johnson and author of the book, *Soul Sister*, in which
she painted herself Black, I was instrumental in 2001
helping to establish an $800,000 journalism
scholarship in her name at the Howard University
School of Communication.

Artis Hampshire Cowan, Esq., Senior Vice
President, Secretary, Board of Trustees, Howard
University, wrote this to me in a proclamation to me:

> Howard University is extremely proud to pay
> tribute to public relations guru, Ofield Dukes. While
> Dukes is a journalism graduate of Wayne State
> University, yet is a beloved son of Howard whose
> illustrious, pioneering career has inured to the
> benefit of the University for over 40 years.
>
> The mutual love affairs Ofield Dukes and the
> Capstone began in 1971, with the launching of the
> HU School of Communications (now the John H.
> Johnson School of Communications). Dukes was not
> only instrumental in formulating the public relations
> curriculum, but also served as an adjunct professor in
> PR for 25 years, and is credited with influencing
> hundreds of African-American students to enter the
> field. A staunch advocate for both public relations
> and Howard, Dukes, working closely with the School
> of Communications Dean, launched his own
> fundraising campaign, which resulted in some 40 of
> his former students pledging $10,009 to their Alma
> Mater.

Outside of the classroom, Dukes donned another cap as public relations counsel to three Howard University presidents—James Cheek, Franklyn Jenifer, and H. Patrick Swygert, and the HU Board of Trustees. Howard leadership has sought his invaluable and expert advice in strategic communications and in crisis management situations.

We at Howard are extremely proud of our long and fruitful association with this "quiet giant," who remains a vital advisor and practitioner to this day.

Recognition by Public Relations Profession

On the third day of January in 2001, I was called by Katherine Lewton, newly elected national president of the Public Relations Society of America (PRSA), urging me to accept the first chairmanship of a task force to promote minority diversity in the PR industry.[92] I accepted the challenge.

As chairman of the PRSA Task Force on Diversity, I developed a mission statement, and for three years traveled thousands of miles across the country carrying a message of diversity as a smart business strategy, in light of a racially, culturally and

---

[92] PRSA had other committees and sections dedicated to minority affairs, multicultural communication before 2001; however, in 2001, the task force Dukes led was given the label diversity and a new precise charge.

ethnically diverse market place. I spoke at public relations conferences and before public relations chapters and my message was generally well received. I devoted a lot of time and work to this special effort.

In recognition of my leadership, Kathy Lewton sent me this statement:

> In 2000, when I became president-elect of the Public Relations Society of America, and thought about the issues facing our profession, I knew I needed to seek out and involve a key cadre of industry leaders who could assist the Society in addressing these issues. I need leader/advisers who could focus on a specific issue, but also had broad vision, seeing the big picture of what PR professionals needed, and also were well known and respected throughout out industry.
>
> One issue we were grappling with was diversity— rather, the lack of diversity in the PR profession, identifying a respected leader to help with that issue was probably the easiest task of my presidency.
>
> I called Ofield Dukes.
>
> Busier than ever, involved in a myriad of client projects and commitments to not-for-profit organizations and causes, Ofield answered promptly.
>
> "Of course, I'll help. What can I do?"
>
> Vintage Ofield Dukes. When needed, he never says no!

In 2001, Ofield chaired our Diversity Task Force, and his leadership and assistance were invaluable.

By his very presence as a senior counselor to me and to the PRSA Board, Ofield extended his credibility to our association.

He helped us address issues relating to attracting more diverse membership, meeting the needs of those members, and to better positioning PRSA as an organization truly committed to diversity. He not only helped us create program that staff and volunteers executed, including a much bigger focus on broadening membership at the local chapter level, but also was available on an 'on-call' basis whenever I had a concern or the Board need his wise counsel. And we didn't just turn to Ofield on diversity issues; he also helped up develop our positions on a variety of challenges facing the profession.

The most important thing that Ofield did for PRSA—and by extension, our profession—was to make diversity a true commitment, not just an 'add on' one-year-emphasis. He helped imprint a commitment to diversity into our organizational DNA, and in subsequent years, PRSA diversity programs have grown and blossomed from the seeds he planted.

Late in 2001, Ofield was honored with PRSA's Gold Anvil, the highest award given by the Society, recognizing his lifetime of professional achievements. I was thrilled to be able to present the award to Ofield at our annual International

Conference, and to thank him for helping PRSA
become a diversity-centric organization.

Impact of PRSA Gold Anvil Award

Harold Burson, the founder of Burson-
Marsteller, one of the largest PR firms in the world,
joined Kathy Lewton, national president of PRSA, in
presenting me with the Gold Anvil, a momentous
moment in my professional career.

Countless awards and ceremonies of celebration
followed that presentation. However, one was most
meaningful, a luncheon in Washington, D.C.,
attended by more than 800 friends and supporters.
At that luncheon, Cathy Hughes, founder of Radio
One, announced establishing a scholarship in my
name at the Howard University School of
Communications. She added that she would be
hosting a special ceremony in Detroit to name the
headquarters of her three radio stations there in my
honor. That ceremony was held in Detroit in May
2002.

Return Visit to Alabama

In 2003, I was privileged to receive an invitation
from the Dean of the School of Communications at
the University of Alabama for a lecture before several

hundreds of their communication students and to be honored by the Dean at a special luncheon.[93] I was treated as a VIP. Oh, how times had changed. And it took the University of Alabama's celebrated football coach, Bear Bryant until the 1950s to have courage to go against southern tradition by recruiting Black football players. What a journey from the cotton fields of Crenshaw County in rural Alabama to the once racially segregated hallowed halls of the University of Alabama.

World Bank Ofield Dukes Scholarship Fund

Thelma Jones, World Bank, honored Dukes through establishing a partnership with Howard University students to help diversify banking communications professionals. She wrote this announcing the scholarship:

> I am pleased to have been involved as an official of the World Bank in establishing for the first time the Ofield Dukes Scholarship Fund for students from the Howard University John H. Johnson School of Communications. Several of the top students from Howard University (will gain) valuable experience at the World Bank as recipients of the

---

[93].Video from his visit is available on the Plank Center for Leadership in Public Relations website http://plankcenter.ua.edu/resources/leaders/videos/

Ofield Dukes Scholarship Fund. This was a milestone at the World Bank and a confirmation of his professionalism and commitment to Howard University PR students.

A Top PRWeek *Communicator of the Year—2005*

The December 15, 2005, *PRWeek*, the main PR industry trade publication, named me one of the top five communicators of the year, along with Max Mayfield, Director of the National Hurricane Center; Marsha Evans, president of the American Red Cross; Steve Jobs, CEO of Apple; Dan Senor, Vice President of Global Communications Strategy for Google; and Senator Mary Landrieu, of Louisiana.

PRWeek wrote that "Ofield Dukes, the longtime PR pro and president of the Black Public Relations Society of Washington, D.C., spearheaded an examination of the industry's struggle to embrace diversity in the workplace. Through his leadership in bringing people together, the industry finally made some progress in 2005."

The Gold Anvil Award and national *PRWeek* recognition pushed me back toward the top of the mountain in my public relations career. And having gone through a midnight period made me a better and stronger person, with a greater sense of humility and thanks to the source of my spiritual faith and strength, God. This proves a simple point in life, you can be down but not out. After a long, dark midnight, there remains hope that morning will come and the sun will shine, possibly brighter than ever.

A Second Marriage

In my youth, I was told by my father, if you fail the first time, try harder the next time. This could have been a motivation in my second marriage. The marriage was not planned. It just happened after a series of social events with a long-time friend, Elaine Robinson Sutton, a crown jewel from Richmond, Virginia.

Elaine and her then husband, Dr. Valvin Sutton, Jr., were my special friends and neighbors while he did his medical residency at Howard University Hospital. I would babysit for their son, Valvin III.

Years after they moved back to their home town of Richmond, regrettably, they ended up going through a difficult divorce.

It was after that divorce that on one special occasion that Elaine called to invite me, as an old platonic friend, to be her escort at her daughter's Debutante Ball in Richmond. I gladly agreed. One social invitation led to a series of others.

On August 3, 1991, we were married in an
elegant ceremony in downtown Richmond, under a
gazebo, overlooking the historic James River. For 10
years, I commuted to Richmond on the weekend and
all holidays to be with my wife. We enjoyed each
other's company and made trips to London, Paris,
Cape Town Johannesburg, South Africa, on boat
cruises, among others.

In long-term human relations, things happened,
unexpected things. Small differences evolve and
become exaggerated if unattended. Elaine, in her
retirement as an assistant public-school principal,
looked forward to my retirement with her in
Richmond. She had a beautiful home in suburban
Richmond.

Deep down, the pseudo-society and provincial
political climate of Richmond did not appeal to me.
And I wrestled with that thought. And I think
somehow the physical and mental wear and tear of
driving 200 miles round trip to Richmond every
weekend must have had some impact.

It really pained me and even more pained and
disappointed Elaine when I decided that we should
terminate our marital commitment and remain the
best of friends. This was of great disappointment to
Elaine. However, we have remained very good
friends. During the 2010 series of health challenges,
Elaine had her daughter, Valeta, to bring food to me

on several occasions. I remember Valeta telling me that, "Ofield, we still consider you an important member of our family."

There is no value that you can place on enduring friendship.

The Aging Process—2010 Health Challenges— A God-inspired Miracle

After more than 77 years of good health, and playing tennis, singles, throughout the years, I was confronted in January of 2010 with an unexpected health problem. But it really should not have been "unexpected" because we have a tendency to ignore symptoms of the aging process for those of us fortunate to live that long. It is inevitable that physical conditions of the boy will decline, and strange pains will occur.

I was really surprised when my doctor at Kaiser Permanente called and indicated that my kidney was not performing up to par and she would monitor it. Over a period of time, my kidney became worse.

It was in June of 2010 that I received an urgent call from Dr. Devika S. Wijesekera, of the Nephrology section at Kaiser Permanente Medical Center. She needed for me to come in for an important consultation. I met with her the next day. Dr. Wijesekera checked the computer carrying my comprehensive medical data. She said I had a chronic kidney disease stage 3. My kidney was deteriorating to an almost fatal 10 percent, and I had to make a decision. Having a transplant, at my age, was out of the question. The only other alternative was entering dialysis.

I decided to do that in June. I had to go to the Washington Hospital Center for the preparation for dialysis. I began dialysis, getting up at 5:30 a.m. and going in for dialysis at the center three days a week—Tuesday, Thursday, and Saturday, from 6:30 a.m. to 10:30 a.m.

This was a difficult interruption in one's life style and work schedule. After dialysis, my energy level was affected, so was my appetite, and my body strength was reduced. But I needed to have a positive attitude about the change. And for that reason, I waited to share my health problem with my daughter, Roxi, in Baton Rouge, and my sisters and other family members.

At the same time, in July, my left arm became paralyzed, and I found myself driving my car and doing everything else with my right arm. After a visit with a Kaiser orthopedic surgeon, I underwent a surgical procedure on my left arm.

It was not until the later part of August that I felt comfortable in sharing with my daughter my acute kidney problem and my being in dialysis. So, I flew to Baton Rouge and in a very positive way shared what was a new life style, of having my life saved through dialysis. She calmly accepted my explanation.

Upon my return to Washington, I shared the information with my family. Since I had no family and relatives in Washington, my three sisters were ready to come to Washington to take care of "their dear brother." I insisted that was not necessary. As a compromise, they all agreed to send food care packages.

It was one Sunday afternoon in October when my telephone rang. Surprisingly, it was my wonderful doctor, Dr. Wijesekera. Now, why would she be taking time to call me on a Sunday afternoon? She did have me taking periodic blood tests to check on my condition in dialysis and to monitor my failing kidney.

She was quick to speak, "Mr. Dukes, I have good news. You kidney has recovered, and I am removing you from dialysis."

This came as a shock to me because I met people at the dialysis center who had been in dialysis for years and accepted the fact they would be there for the duration of their lives. And I had accepted the same notion. I told my doctor that this was a medical miracle, and that my God had worked this miracle through her. What a great relief!

However, in December, I faced another health challenge. It was a Sunday morning that I tried to leave my bed for early church service. And I could not move my left leg, which was in excruciating pain. In dealing with this problem, I had a series of MRI examinations on my left leg, knee, thigh, spine, and abdomen.

With some improvement, I could walk with a cane and in a Christmas trip to Detroit to visit family, I had to use a wheel chair at both airports because I did not have the leg strength to walk a long distance, not even a short distance.

Doctors reviewed the results of the MRI examinations and said they would continue to monitor my condition.

Presently, I can walk without the cane, without any pain. My strength is back; I have a great appetite, and I feel so blessed to be able to continue my work in the exciting field of public relations, my 42nd year. What a blessing!

Spiritual Values—A Matter of Faith

At the age of nine, I was baptized at the Church of Our Father in Detroit and from that sacred moment I have had a strong faith in God, resulting in a strong faith in my own ability to deal with adversity.

From my religion, Baptist, and from the bible, I have learned the important message and principle that above all the Christian virtues that God's commandment (St. John 16:12) is "That you love one another, as I have loved you." This is often translated to loving thy neighbor as thyself. And this becomes a difficult challenge in life, just liking people you don't like, not moving to the next phase of love.

I have learned from proverbs that "In all your getting in life get knowledge, wisdom and understanding." This principle has been so important in my personal and business life in helping me to make prudent judgments and not spend in time second-guessing myself.

And from Ecclesiastes, third chapter, I have always been intrigued by the words of the preacher.

To everything there is a season, and a time to every purpose under the heaven. A time to be born, and a time to die, a time to plan, and a time to pluck up that which is planted; A time to kill, and a time to heal; a time to break down, and a time to build up; A time to weep, and a time to laugh; a time to mourn, and a time to dance; A time to cast away stones, and a time to gather stones together; a time to embrace, and a time to refrain from embracing; A time to get, and a time to lose; a time to keep, and a time to cast away; A time to rend, and a time to sew; a time to keep silence, and a time to speak; A time to love, and a time to hate; a time of war, and a time of peace.

From the words of the preacher, we need to understand our purpose in life and what seasons we are moving through. Somehow, I feel we all have a purpose in life, and what a tragedy for those of us who go through life not knowing what that purpose is. Some of us could be guilty of feeling confused about where we are in life, in our youth, in mid-life, or in the twilight of life, not knowing and appreciating the joy and beauty of that season and some understanding of our purpose in life.

I agreed with Milt Albom in his best-selling book, *Have a Little Faith*, that faith is an essential spiritual ingredient of life that is subject to propel us to our highest level of peace, contentment and human existence.

My own faith in God has been a major treasury of my life, my source of inspiration and faith in my own ability to deal with life's frustrations and disappointments. This was confirmed as I went through the serious health challenges of 2010—the kidney failure and five months of kidney dialysis, a paralyzed left arm, and the inability to walk due to excruciating pains in my left leg. I feel that my God worked through the medical genius of my physicians at Kaiser Permanente to create some semblance of a miracle in my recovery.

I now feel so blessed.

My Remaining Mountaintop Experience

When I reflect on my past experiences, I have had not one mountaintop experience but several.

My mountaintop experience was not traveling with Mrs. Coretta Scott King to the enthronement of Archbishop Tutu in Cape Town, South Africa. It was not providing office space for Alex Haley while he was writing his epic book, *Roots* and joining him on his triumphant return to the Village of Juffure in The Gambia.

My mountaintop experience was not standing in my office at the National Press Building at 4 a.m. on a cold wintry January morning as hundreds of buses brought more than 100,000 people to Washington for the first Stevie Wonder March to make Dr. King's birthday a national holiday.

It was my becoming a parent with the birth of Roxi and her entering my bedroom during my darkest hour to say, simply, "Daddy I love you."

The second mountaintop experience was that hot, summer day in August 2001 when I received a surprising call that the Public Relations Society of America has awarded me its Gold Anvil.

The third mountaintop experience came on a Mother's Day in 2009 when my ex-wife, Rosa, hosted a cookout for my daughter and her husband

and my two-year-old grandson, Michael Dukes Victorian.

When my daughter and her husband arrived at her mother's house in Fort Washington, Maryland, my grandson hopped out of the car, and ran toward me with his arms outreached...and shouted..."Poppa Dukes...Poppa Dukes!" He then jumped into my arms, hugged me, kissed me on the cheek...and said, "Poppa Dukes, Poppa Dukes, I love you. I love you."

And that moment was, indeed, my third mountaintop experience.

XXII.

Lessons from Life's Journey

For me, along life's difficult journey, many people were sources of encouragement, inspiration and support and I firmly believe my success has been based on how well I have learned and heeded lessons from these sources. Many of my lessons came from the following sources that helped me along a long, challenging but eventful journey.

My parents: Violet and Garfield Dukes: A strong Christian faith, the many unspoken manifestations of their love and their abiding philosophy of treating others as you want to be treated;

My sisters, the late Arlene Brown, Lou Brock, Anne Harris, and Betty Hayden: Their love and humility to prevent me from becoming a spoiled only son;

Roxi Trapp-Dukes Victorian, as my daughter: Her roots of deep love and endless joy and priorities challenges of being a devoted parent;

Roxi Victorian (my daughter) and her husband, Michael: The mutual love, joy, social and intellectual compatibility in their marriage, and excitement of being parents;

Michael Dukes Victorian, my four-year-old grandson: The joy and beauty of his youthful love;

Clarence Shelley, former high school mate and former Dean, University of Illinois: strong faith in the potential of Southside Chicago students in greatest need;

Michigan Chronicle Editor-General Manager Longworth M. Quinn: Remaining calm in the most stressful circumstances and need to be an excellent writer;

Dr. James J. McClendon, President of Detroit NAACP: a commitment to civil rights and public service;

Sonia Porter (Thompson), Vice President of the Young Adult Division of the Detroit NAACP: The strength of loyal support and an enduring friendship;

Attorney Hobart Taylor, General Counsel to President Lyndon B. Johnson: Having a strategic vision and being prepared for any new opportunity;

Louis Martin, Advisor to Presidents John F. Kennedy, Lyndon B. Johnson and Jimmy Carter, and a co-founder of the *Michigan Chronicle*: Becoming a student of the art and challenge of national politics;

Vice President Hubert H. Humphrey: Having a happy disposition and passion for one's work, especially public service;

President Lyndon B. Johnson: An ardent practitioner of philosopher William James' theory of pragmatism. For President Johnson, the art of life and politics was to pursue the ideal and achieve the probable; I adopted his 10 principles of public relations;

Dr. Leon Sullivan, of Philadelphia, who led the fight to end apartheid in South Africa and founder of the job development program, OIC: Courageous, visionary leadership;

LeBaron Taylor, Vice President of Sony Music Entertainment and pioneer in the promotion of Black music in the recording industry: A generous soul who gave so much too so many in his dedication to the cause of Black people, and who also placed the highest value on friendship;

Dr. Rosa Trapp-Dail, ex-wife: an extraordinary friendship;

Alex Haley, author of *Roots*: Intense commitment to the history, culture and heritage of African Americans and the great patience in writing his book;

Mrs. Coretta Scott King, President of the Martin Luther King, Jr. Committee on Non-Violent Social Change: The essence of grace and pure humility;

Dr. C. Delores Tucker, founder of the National Congress of Black Women Chair of the Democratic

National Committee's Black Caucus: genuine friendship and a lady of great determination and courage;

Musician Stevie Wonder: a talented, kindhearted soul dedicated to the cause of his people;

Dr. Dorothy Irene Height, Chair, and National Council of Negro Women: her brilliant mind, strategic thinking, and strong dedication to work and the cause of Black people were legendary;

Congressman Charles Rangel, first Black Chairman of the House Ways and Means Committee: A lifetime of dedication to public service at a personal sacrifice;

Congressman Charles Diggs, Jr., Founder, first Chairman of Congressional Black Caucus: A man of progressive vision and courage of his convictions;

Ronald Brown, first Black Chairman of the Democratic National Committee: A remarkable organizer, brilliant political strategist, who was calm under the most difficult challenges and circumstances;

Cathy Hughes, of Washington, D.C., founder, Radio and TV One: Intense determination to overcome difficult challenges;

Rev. Unnia Pettus, Ph.D.: the remarkable faith in her God during an endless stream of near death health challenges; the deep, unflinching faith described by Mitch Albom in his bestselling book, *Have a Little Faith*;

Poet Kahil Gibran, in his book, *The Prophet*, the true, pure meaning of friendship;

Dale Carnegie and his "public relations bible" on *The Art of Winning Friends and Influencing People;*

Dr. Norman Vincent Peale, *The Power of Positive Thinking;*

Greek Philosophers Socrates and Aristotle, Discovering the true essence of who you are;

Proverbs: In all your getting in life, get knowledge, wisdom and understanding;

Jesus Christ: An abiding faith and finding a way to love thy neighbor as thyself.

Twenty-Five Principles of Success

1. Strong family support
2. Adoption of strong social and spiritual values and ethics
3. Passion for excellence
4. Strong work ethic—no substitute for hard work
5. Self-awareness, deep self-appreciation
6. High self-esteem and self confidence
7. Patience
8. Perseverance
9. Genuine Humility

10. Faith in one's ability to deal with adversity, obstacles, without excuses
11. Faith in God
12. Intense determination to succeed
13. Trust in my judgment to seek the best knowledge, wisdom and understanding (Proverbs, third chapter)
14. Positive attitude
15. Emphasis on interpersonal relations—practice of Golden Rule
16. Evolving definitive career vision of professional goals
17. Calm temperament to prevent stress
18. Exceptional mentoring and genuine, supportive friendships
19. Maturity—educational growth outside of classroom
20. Reaching out to be kind, of assistance and respectful to other
21. Commitment to giving back to community, teaching, community service, civil rights involvement
22. Preparation to take advantage of new and equal opportunities
23. Actively maintaining physical health through recreational activity—tennis; healthy habits, lifestyle

24. Placing the highest values on being a parent and a meaningful and productive family life contributing to peace of mind

25. Always seeking internal peace and happiness.

XXIII.

Letters of Note

Over the years, I collected letters and emails from leaders, clients, colleagues and students. Here is a sample of some of those messages.

To Ofield Dukes, (November 19, 1976)
I really appreciate your effort in getting out the vote. Without your hard work, the results could have been quite different.

—(President-elect) Jimmy Carter

* * *

To Ofield Dukes, (September 27, 1979)
Thank you for serving on the recent Trade Mission to Africa headed by Ambassador Andrew Young. I appreciate your contribution to the success of the trip, and I am pleased to send you my best wishes.

—President Jimmy Carter

* * *

Ofield, (July 11, 1978)
On behalf of all of us associated with the Bullets, thank you for the tremendous job you did in

originating and coordinating our special day in
Washington.

The time was unbelievably short—the task
beyond that which any one person could handle; and,
yet, you did it all and brought it off so magnificently.
It created for all of us a day that we shall never
forget—one that gave our championship victory a
meaning and now a memory that will live with all of
us forever. On behalf of all of us associated with the
Bullets, thank you for a superior effort and a job well
done.

—Jerry Sachs, President,
Washington Bullets

* * *

Dear Ofield, (August 9, 1994)
I would like to extend a personal thanks to you
for taking the time to assist me in developing a
public relations strategy for the multi-year fiscal plan.
Your advice and robust discussion has been most
helpful. As a result, I was able to incorporate several
of your ideas. Thank you.

—Sharon Pratt Kelly, Mayor,
Government of the District of
Columbia

* * *

Dear Ofield, (November 29, 1977)

Just a note of special thanks for your help in making my recent testimonial dinner a tremendous success. The dinner was the highlight of a day that I shall long remember with pride and humility.

—Benjamin L. Hooks,
Executive Director, NAACP

* * *

Dear Ofield, (September 21, 1988)

I extend my congratulations over the very fine job you performed in arranging the Salute to Justice Thurgood Marshall. I know something of the difficulties under which you were working and I admire the patience and understanding that you exhibited.

—Wiley A. Branton. Esq.

* * *

Dear Ofield, (June 11, 1981)

While somewhat elated, I did want to put pen in hand and say thanks for your assistance during the early start-up days of my firm. Your time and guidance made a difference.

—Alexis Herman, Vice President,
Green-Herman & Associates

* * *

Dear Ofield, (July 8, 1996)
Thanks for your 5 June 1997 memo. You do
good work.

—Harold Ickes, Assistant to the
President (Bill Clinton) and Deputy
Chief of Staff, the White House

* * *

Ofield, (October 14, 1996)
Thank you for your good work—22 days to go—
keep it up.

—Donald L. Fowler, Chair,
Democratic National Committee

* * *

Dear Ofield, (October 1, 1986)
I want to express my personal thanks to you for
your support and contribution during the time
preceding our departure, while we were in southern
Africa and since our return.

—Coretta Scott King, President, the
Martin Luther King, Jr. Center for
Nonviolent Social Change, Inc.

* * *

Dear Ofield, (October 1, 1986)
Thanks a lot for your generosity of your time yesterday. You still are one of the best idea guys around.

> — Rep. Charles C. Diggs, Jr., Chair,
> House District committee

* * *

Dear Ofield, (September 11, 1980)
Now that I am out of the hospital, I can respond properly to your warm and comforting letter of July 30th (1960). When you have spent the months that I have spent in a hospital bed, there are times when you need to hear words of wisdom and understanding from old friends. Your letter served that need and I want you to know how deeply I appreciate it. Most certainly it was not a routine get well message, although they also serve to cheer and comfort, but rather an expression of your own thoughts done with eloquence and compassion.

> —Vernon E. Jordan, Jr., President,
> National Urban League

* * *

Dear Ofield, (April 22, 1976)
Thank you so much for you contribution to my
re-election campaign. I deeply appreciate your
support and continued confidence in me.
　　　　　　　　　—Senator Hubert H. Humphrey

*　*　*

Dear Mr. Dukes,
Let me once again express my sincere
appreciation for our assistance with the Signing
Ceremony on March 14, (1998) involving the United
State Agency for International Development and my
Foundation, the International Foundation for
Education and Self-Help. From my perspective, this
was indeed a momentous occasion resulting in the
continuation of this partnership which will make
possible the placement of an additional two hundred
teachers from the United States in African countries,
the training of two hundred African bankers, and the
continuation of our effective Debt for Development
program. I shall always be grateful for your
encouragement and support.
　　　　　　　　　—Leon H. Sullivan, President,
　　　　　　　　　International Foundation for
　　　　　　　　　Education and Self-Help

*　*　*

Dear Ofield, (November 16, 1998)
The headlines said it all. The only thing left to be said is "Thank you!" Your hard work resulted in African-American voters increasing their share of the electorate from six percent in 1994 to 11 percent this year (1998). The time, creativity and effort you gave to our Get-Out-The-Vote project made a real difference in specific races and in the political landscape of the country. I greatly appreciate your friendship and support. We accomplished a lot and laid the groundwork to finally take back the House.
    —Rep. Charles B. Rangel

* * *

Howard University and American University Student comments

Linda Sanders-Hawkins, Director of Admissions, Howard University:
Mr. Dukes, I knew when I was in your class and you gave me the opportunity to intern with you at the National Press Building. I shared with my children my involvement through your office on the historical impact of making Dr. King's birthday a national holiday. I will always be grateful to you for your generosity and mentoring. My professional accomplishments as well as my ability to serve at Howard are due in part to you.

* * *

Robin E. Beaman, President, Beaman, Inc., Chicago, Illinois:

Mr. Dukes, the consummate PR executive, brought all that wisdom to the classroom and we loved it when he shared stories that complemented what we were learning in our textbook. He cared about all his students and expected nothing less than our best work, yet his star students landed the prime internships. He taught us that excellent writing and communication skills were a must and integrity was everything.

"His wisdom propelled me to great heights in my career. I had the privilege of managing public relations of America's three African-American billionaires—Sheila Johnson, Robert Johnson and Oprah Winfrey. Inspired by Mr. Dukes, I launched my own public relations and advertising firm in 1996 in Chicago. Throughout my career and even today I call him for professional guidance and his advice is always dead-on. Howard University is an oasis of great professors from around the world and Mr. Dukes was one of the rarest treasures. I have been blessed to know Mr. Dukes and to call him my teacher, mentor and friend.

* * *

Lynne Scott Jackson, Distinguished Lecturer, The City College of New York:
For more than 30 years, I have known Mr. Dukes as a professor, mentor, and fellow PR practitioner. During my days at Howard University, he asked us to verbally introduce ourselves to classmates; a class assignment or so we thought. I responded with a list of college activities. His response: "Ms. Scott, you relayed what you do, but no one really cares about that. Who are you? What do you stand for?"

I have never forgotten that lesson as I relate to diverse audiences and continue to hone my craft as a counselor and educator. Realizing the importance of practical experience, Howard University PR students were among the first interns to work behind the scenes during the formative years of the Congressional Black Caucus Foundation Annual Legislative Conference, thanks to Mr. Dukes. A class visit to his office was eye opening and made me realize I didn't just want a career in PR. I wanted to be a powerhouse consultant like Mr. Dukes.

* * *

Sonia Osinloye, former Vice President (2001–2010), Fleishman-Hillard Public Relations Firm, alumna, Howard University School of Communication, 1990:

As a young public relations student, from the
moment I stepped into Professor Dukes' classroom,
I knew that I was embarking on an enlightening
educational journey and that he would leave an
indelible impression upon my life. From his thought,
solid understand of public relations to his genuine
care for his students and others, he has been a
mentor and a pillar of support and encouragement
long after I have left his classroom and I am grateful.
An amazing PR expert, an amazing man.

* * *

Stephanie Bluma, former deputy assistant
administrator for public affairs, USAID Deputy Asst.
Administrator for Public Affairs (1997–98, The
American University):
Dear Mr. Dukes,
As a student in your International Public
Relations class, I would like to extend to you my
thanks for the time you invested in our class. Your
personal knowledge of public relations added a great
deal of perspective to the theoretical models that we
studied.
Additionally, the career sessions you offered
were very beneficial, and certainly offered me
direction as I embark on my career.

* * *

Tracey Pinson, former director, Office of Small Business Programs, Office of the Secretary of the U.S. Army:

When I was fifteen years old, my first job was with Ofield Dukes & Associates. My experience there was invaluable and contributes significantly to who I am today. For that I am truly grateful.

*   *   *

Index

A

B

Y

Z

CPSIA information can be obtained
at www.ICGtesting.com
Printed in the USA
BVHW04s1926290318
511907BV00004BA/5/P

9 780999 024515